EFFORTLESS PROVISION

Where Survival Ends and A Divine Encounter With Inspiration Begins

John C. Meyer

End of Effort Media

Effortless Provision is dedicated to all those who decide it's time to make the shift from HARD work to creative flow.

CONTENTS

INTRODUCTION

As far back as I can remember I watched the people I love work hard for what they have. As a young boy, I remember watching my dad climb into his truck early in the morning to drive deep into the woods to cut down the trees he would need to make a living as a logger. The years would pass, and I witnessed the same as he drove cross-country to deliver a variety of freight to the east coast. I remember thinking, "Man, my dad is the hardest working man I know!". I was proud of the fact he was a great provider and a hard worker. My mom was the same. She worked just as hard, if not harder raising myself and two sisters. I love them dearly. They did a great job raising us to respect others, go out and live our dreams, and love God with our entire being. I respect and love them for the integrity, work ethic, and godly principles they instilled in us. I just simply had more questions when it came to the subjects of work and provision as a whole.

I really didn't think there was anything innately wrong with working hard, because it's all I was used to. I mean, after all, much of society is wired to work hard in a variety of occupations and industries. But as I grew older and began working in industries and jobs I didn't like; I began to question this thing called "efforted work".

It wasn't until I reached the ripe old age of 27 and had a major encounter with God through a set of challenging events, that I really began to question it. Not because I thought work was bad, but because the word "hard" was attached to it. I began to ask God things like, *"Why does work have to be hard?"* and *"If work is good, then why do I feel frustrated when I'm doing some of it?"* and *"Why does it seem the harder I work, the less I get paid?"* and *"Why do I always seem to struggle with this money thing?"* and *"Why does work have to take the life out of people?"* and *"Why does the call of HARD work have to rip families apart?"* and *"Was this what you originally had in mind for humanity?".* On and on the list of questions grew.

Again, I wasn't raised to be lazy, so that wasn't the reason for all the questions. It was more of a desire to see if there was in fact, a better or "higher" way to look at work and this wonderful thing we call provision.

After coming to the end of myself, I am happy to report there is a higher way. ***Effortless Provision*** is more than a message of hope and freedom. It's an actual encounter with the happy, non-religious Jesus walking me through the heart of humanity, and the effortless flow of Heaven's provision.

Every time I sat down to write it's like he stepped through my very being to think, feel, converse, and type with me.

There are answers in this book I have wanted to know my entire adult life regarding God's true nature, and how provision operates from Heaven's perspective. It took me approx. two years to dictate this very conversation because it has taken me two years and longer to mature into living what is written on these pages.

So, to all those who have ever struggled with frustration, depression, anger, mundane work, lack, poverty, and self-effort, this "living" book is for you. It is my life message and a "thorn in the flesh" if you will, when it comes to understanding effortless provision.

My prayer is that you will posture yourself in such a way that will allow you to receive this encounter/message without bias. I would ask that you take off any conditioned, negative reactions and religious lenses you may have. Set them aside, and receive what Jesus wants to say to you inside these pages. If you do, I promise you will receive something that will change your life for the better.

You will see Jesus in a way that will cause you to rethink some things because you will experience him sharing from a place of relatability and authenticity. It's the Jesus you always knew to be true away from the effort found in religion.

Piles of blessings on you as you absorb what you are about to read. Much love and abundance!

Here's to the end of effort.

Your friend, John

ENTER THE STAIRWAY

As soon as I sat down and closed my eyes in my favorite chair this morning, my eyes were opened to see into the spirit realm. I saw what looked like a transparent staircase suspended in mid-air above a beach going straight up into the Heavens. I knew this was a familiar place because it felt warm and peaceful. I soon realized where I was standing. I had been there before in the natural. I was standing on a beach in Hawaii, my beloved home. (*It was all so clear and tangible that it felt like I was actually there in body and spirit.*)

While I stood in the warmth of the sand looking at this beautiful, transparent stairwell, I thought, "Why am I seeing these steps hanging over the shoreline in Hawaii?" As soon as I had the thought, it came to me instantly. They were there because it's my "Happy place" in the natural and in the spirit. There's nothing quite like being in a place where you feel God's presence in your own unique way. The islands are like an open portal to Heaven to me, and actually, it was. God was opening up access this morning to reveal something significant. I could just sense it.

As I stood looking at this beautiful stairwell, I heard a voice, a familiar one, it was Jesus. He said, "Go ahead and climb up, it's not far. It's only twenty-five steps." I thought to myself, hmmm, now why did he say, "Twenty-five steps?" As soon as I thought that He answered with a chuckle. He said, "Because it's easier than you think to "climb" into Mt. Heaven. Come on up I want to show you many wonderful things."

I began counting as I made my way up. With each step I kept thinking of how gorgeous these see-through stairs were. I could see the beautiful blue Hawaii waters below as I climbed and thought this alone is enough. I could stand here forever.

One, two, three, four...I counted as if it was the "climb" that would change my life forever. You see, this was huge for me, because up until this point I had never seen anything like this before in the spirit. Especially, as it pertained to such a specific geographical location. Yes, I have always known that Hawaii is like a modern day "Garden of Eden" because of its natural beauty, people, aloha, music, and rich history permeating her "soil". But this was a whole new level in the spirit.

I took another step and when I got to the top of step number twenty-one there was a stair landing. It looked to be approx. 6' x 6' in diameter. While I stood there for a moment pondering what this landing was for, Jesus answered my thoughts. He said, "Twenty-one is an important year for many people. It's a "Landing point" of growth and transformational choice in their lives. Someone decides to either take the greater plunge into self-efforted ambition as adults or they chose to engage the scroll of Heavens plan".

I thought, you know, he is definitely right about that. I began thinking about my own life and wanted to move quickly on to the next four steps of discovery.

The amazing part about the platform at the twenty first step was that it was still transparent, beautiful, and filled with peaceful glory. It was as if to say, Gods ways and plans never change. They are constant. It's how we choose to look at important steps along the journey of our lives is what really matters. In other words, our steps are transparent and beautiful when we land on the internal stairwell of Heavens well-being through the choices we make. It was a moment I took to heart as I placed my foot on the twenty second step.

Just as soon as I thought about the twenty third step, I broke through a thin layer of clouds into another realm. I stepped into the literal Kingdom of another world. It was Heaven. I felt tangible love, with a capital "L". I soon discovered the twenty-fifth step was the entry point to the "courtyard" of Heaven.

◆ ◆ ◆

The Mountain Of Love

As I stepped in, I heard the words, "Isaiah 25." I just knew I had entered the opening of what some call Zion, but Jesus calls Heaven, the mountain of his presence.

My mind was reeling. This is so different than what everyone was telling me about it or what I thought Mt. Zion was through scripture reading. From what I've read about Zion, I pictured it to be either Jerusalem or a "Mt. Everest" type of mountain some-where. I was wondrously surprised that it was neither! *(Not that I have any problem thinking it was literal Jerusalem, but we all have our own mental pictures of what we think things are like due to the paradigm and maturity level we are in, right?)*

Nevertheless, I was elated at the sight. My "climb" up the stairs was nowhere near the ascent I believed I would have to "climb" to see such a magnificent place. I wasn't out of breath, my legs didn't burn, and I wasn't breathing hard trying to "get in" or "climb up" to see. It was in fact, effortless.

As I stood there to take it all in, I noticed my shoes were standing in what looked and felt like liquid. I couldn't tell right off what was surrounding my feet due to the cloud or "fog" covering the entire "floor" I was standing on. The top landing of the stairwell was spectacular, it seemed to go on forever. It's like I was stand-ing on the very floor of an endless Heaven. I was in awe. Then, I felt a breeze come around my feet and ankles. I looked down and noticed the fog beginning to dissapate. Just as soon as the area around my feet cleared, I was delighted to see the "liquid" I was feeling was gold; pure, beautiful, gold, drenching my feet.

Now, this too was quite different than what I imagined the streets of gold in Heaven to be like. I pictured them to be solid, and transparent, but not liquid. This gold was alive and filled with movement. It was as if it was dancing about my feet and splashing in wave like form all throughout Heaven. It was breathtaking. Especially, when I watched it drip off my shoe like Rain-X windshield wash does on the windshield of a car. It was just like that. The gold would bead up and roll off my shoes, leaving them completely dry. (I was laughing because it was just like God to do something like that for his friends. I don't know about you, but I get a kick out of those kinds of things.)

As I stood there fixated on the gold, I was then immediately transported back "down" to the sandy beach. When I looked back up to where I was a second before, I saw Jesus standing there. He smiled, knelt down, and picked something up straight off the "floor" of Heaven. He took it and started forming it with both hands, sort of like you would do with a ball of clay or a lump of snow. When he finished forming it, it looked like he was getting ready to throw it down to me. (Now, when I say "down" I don't mean that in a literal sense. It's not like the spirit realm is up or down because it surrounds our very lives. It just looked like the steps were above the beach and now I was standing "below" the top of the stairs where Jesus stood.)

◆ ◆ ◆

The Omnipresence Of Heaven

Heaven is merely a breath away. We are in fact eternal beings housed in an earth-bound body that is subjected to gravity. We believe Heaven is up in the sky somewhere, only because we've been taught that it is. It most certainly is in the way the entire cosmos is above, below, and surrounding the earth. But in reality, Heaven lays within and around us. Eternity is in our hearts, but it's also what we are made of internally. We are one with Christ and He is the very substance of Heaven. Just like love has no ending, and you cannot tell where it is dimensionally, so it is with Heaven. We feel love and we experience it all day, every day, whether we are aware of it or not. It's the same with Heaven. We cannot escape its reality. We may not see it with our physical eyes, but the truth is it's the realm in which we find our being as children made in its very image.

As I watched Jesus joyfully turning his hands back and forth molding some kind of substance, flashes of golden light began to flood the sky. I could now see what he was forming. Jesus stood there holding a molded gold bar in his right hand with a huge smile on his face. He paused before tossing it to me. That beautiful smile on that radiant face of his was letting me know that what was about to happen next was going to be a fun ride. He wanted me to see that he was fully enjoying this experience before he tossed the gold to me.

It's like time stood still for a while as Jesus held the gold in his hand. I could feel the gravity of this moment, and knew it was important because he was showing me that it was his heartfelt pleasure to give me a tangible part of the Kingdom.

Woosh...Slap!

Just like that, the gold bar hit my hand as I stood there immersed in the warmth of the sand. I thought, wow! Now this is mind blowing in and of itself that Jesus would toss me down a gold bar, but what does this mean exactly, I asked internally. My reasoning started to kick in a little. Doubleminded thoughts began to trickle in. On one hand (The hand I caught the gold with) I was excited, yet at the same time I was wondering what he wanted me to do with it?

My mind was racing. I thought, now if Jesus was smiling as He threw it down to me, either he is super excited about giving me some wealth or there was some kind of lesson in this...ya know what I mean?

◆ ◆ ◆

Love Gives Because That's What Love Does

Why is it that many of us have such a difficult time believing that God would want to give us that kind of provision, without having to sow money or jump through a hoop with some kind of formula attached? It was really starting to sink in for me after all the years of religious conditioning.

What if he wanted to give me a big-fat gold bar just because he wanted to? I know religion talks about how he would if our behavior changes, or we sow enough chunks of money to build up "equity" to see that kind of "return" from Heaven. But what I've come to learn in recent years is that kind of exchange is called "transactionary" relationship or "formula" friendship. In more simple terms, it's called manipulation. It's the, "If I give you something then I expect you to give me something in return" mindset.

But love doesn't work that way. In fact, love doesn't "work" he just is and has always been. That love is a who and that who is unconditional in his response to all things. In other words, because I love my child, I don't tell him he has to give me $10,000 first before I would ever think about giving him a gold bar or any

other good thing for that matter. I give to him because of love…
period.

Now, there is such a thing as natural timing on some things,
but it doesn't mean I am not excited to give it to him leading up
to that appointed time. And do you know when that eternally
appointed time is? It is now, because we our spirit dwells in the
now. It is given to us in the spirit realm the moment we ask.
Then love manifests it when it's time to happen in the natural
through the alignment of readiness.

Think about the car you dream of giving your child when they
are old enough to drive. When a parent adores their child, they
dream of getting the car way ahead of the appointed time. It is
"given" in the spirit of the mind the moment they dream it up.
Now, they understand full well their child isn't ready to drive
when they're six years old, but they get excited to dream with
their child long before they are old enough to drive a vehicle.
The excitement comes when? Now. That is when the clock starts
ticking towards the appointed time of giving it in the natural because it was birthed in the spirit first through joy.

◆ ◆ ◆

Joy Is The Substance That Attracts

*"Joy in the now is the spiritual strength that
gives birth to an eventual manifestation
of something good in the natural."*

The key is to hold your steady gaze upon his magnificent smile knowing that all good things are on their way. Not because we know through head knowledge, but because joy is our inheritance every moment of every day no matter what is going on. When we posture ourselves this way and allow rest to permeate our mind and emotions, that is when it gets really fun. It's when maturity accelerates, and gratitude begins to act like a magnetic pull for everything good to come into our reality.

The opposite is true when we try to figure out how it will happen, when it will occur, who will bring it, and then try to work for it when it doesn't come at the time of our choosing.

Our self-effort then begins to put up a wall of resistance to the point of frustration, and when frustration takes hold, we begin to blur his smile. This is when we say things like, "This isn't working! I have to work hard for my money or I won't eat! I need to get out and find a higher paying job, so I can get what I want when I want it…like right now!" When all along joyful patience and the gaze were all that were "necessary" to see the trickle, the flow, and then the torrent of blessing headed directly for us. Notice how I said, "See the trickle" and not "working for the trickle" or "Creating a formula for the trickle" in order for the blessing to come.

No, our "job" is to just see it, then have fun playing and creating things in our garden, studio, computer, garage, office, and elsewhere, until it all begins to manifest when it's supposed to. This is what Jesus meant when he said, "I only see and do what My Father sees and does". What does he see and do? He sees humanity as a beautiful masterpiece of his creation, and he dispenses his goodness on everyone, regardless of who they are. He rains his goodness down on both the pre-believing and the believing, because everyone is made in the image of love. And as he is going about doing great things, he is releasing creativity everywhere he goes, which is a magnet for goodness.

The issue lays in the personal belief of an individual. Some believe they are loved, and others are too bound up with internal wounding to believe they could ever be fully accepted and unconditionally loved. They are too busy feeling shame through judging themselves and others to the point of unworthiness. Sadly, even the believing allows past trauma to cloud their belief about his goodness.

The good news is when we simply turn back to his satisfying smile and remain there, the clogging of the "pipes" begins to clear, and the flow of blessing begins to open up. It's always there. It hasn't moved. It is eternally present. We are the ones who move out of alignment from the flow. We don't have to work some kind of formula for it and we certainly don't have to intercede for long hours trying to get it. Begging is not required. Goodness and provision are just Heavens reality, all the time.

◆ ◆ ◆

Tall, Dark and Ripped

As I deeply pondered these things for more than a minute, I found Jesus sitting next to me on the sand. I must have been deep in thought for a while not to notice Jesus walk down the stairs. Perhaps he didn't. He does have other ways of getting from point A to point B you know. It doesn't really matter how he did, it's the fact that I'm now sitting next to the one who molded and fashioned me into something more valuable than gold.

If you ever find yourself sitting next to him in what seems like a real-life experience in the natural, then you will know that it feels like sitting next to your very best friend who's in a great mood. It's comfortable and warming. It's like you've known each other for eternity *(which in fact you have)*.

As I looked over at Jesus, I noticed he was drawing in the sand with his fingers. It was quite noticeable to me that he didn't look like some scrawny little "white" man we see on paintings hanging in cathedral halls or on dining room walls. No, not at all. If I could describe Him to you in this realm of life, I would say he looked like a really tan or dark-skinned mix between Thor and Aqua Man. You know, like the actors who played these characters in the movies. *(If you don't know what they look like then google their latest movies and you'll see what I am talking about).*

Now, I'm not necessarily speaking of their exact looks. His physique was more like a silhouette of these guys and his countenance like the humorous side of these actors. He most definitely wasn't scrawny, and He wasn't ugly. He was gorgeous, ripped, and filled with joy. He was like the best friend you always want to hang out with because they are funny, charismatic, kind, safe, strong, empowering, and wise.

The bottom line is he is awesome! Why? Not because he is all of those physical things alone, but because he genuinely knew me. He knew every ounce of who I was and will ever be. It was like he was me. That's how familiar He was and is. He could see right through my stuff and it wasn't intimidating or scary in the least. It was relieving, relaxing, and life changing.

Again, picture in your mind sitting next to your very best friend in the natural. You're having a great time conversing together, when your friend says something that is hilarious. You then fall into one another laughing and crying so hard you feel like you're going to burst! Yeah, we did that as we sat and talked about life with all of its wonder, beauty, adventure, laughter, fun, and satisfaction. We also talked about my petty worries, fears, and concerns about the past, present, and future. The more he looked at me and the more we laughed together, the more the negative things began to fade, and I remembered just how much I love this God of love and the Jesus I never really saw in religion.

I could just sit there in the warm Hawaii sand forever, listening, laughing, and staring at my best friend who knew every part of me. It's as if all of my worries began to vanish the more his presence affected my soul.

Having said all of this, I do realize that some of you may have never known this image and person of Jesus before. Perhaps he has only been a mental source of trauma and abuse to you because of the way he has been portrayed and presented through religious institutional paradigms or spiritual abuse through leadership. For that, my heart breaks for you. I too have fallen prey to an image of God that was more like an angry dictator who couldn't be pleased no matter what you tried to do. I can honestly say I no longer believe that about this glorious God. My spirit always knew he was good, but my trained indoctrination and believe system made my mind believe otherwise. My prayer for you is that the revelation of his goodness hits you like a big fat "gold bar" would hit your bank account at lightning speed. It's just a matter of opening your heart to see him differently.

◆ ◆ ◆

Christ Really Is That Good

"Christ is as good as your spirit knows him to be. He is as safe, loving, kind, and relational as your heartbeat is to your own body. Conditioning makes us believe otherwise."

After we sat in the sand for a while, we stood up and began to walk down the beach. As we walked and talked conversing about many things, Jesus suddenly stopped, turned his body 180 degrees and busted out in a dance move. I started laughing at the site, because I'd never imagine Jesus to dance like that. I loved it.

I watched as he danced a little more before he spun around one last time and then took his right hand and stuck it into the spirit realm to pull out another gold bar. Only this time he held it at one end, looked right at me and said, "Grab the other end." He didn't say anything with physical words. It was more spirit-to-spirit words as he stood there looking at me with that familiar little smirk on his face. I looked down at the gold bar, then right into his eyes and had a deep, supernatural knowing we were joint heirs of all things. A joint heir to the wealth I was holding and the love I was experiencing. I knew with everything in me that what was his was mine. Like we were brothers from the same "Mother" or "Father", but even closer because we were one together. It was an overwhelming feeling of acceptance, love, gratitude, and awe. It was one of safety, comfort, and security, knowing he could pull anything I had "need" of right out of Heaven any time I needed it.

As I stood there overwhelmed by this captivating moment, he took the gold bar, broke it in half with ease and said, "Take the half that is in your hand and pay off your debt. The other half will come to you when your belief joyfully expands to match Heaven's wealth." He then pitched his half of the gold bar back into Heavens realm and it disappeared into thin air. He then looked at me and asked, "Or would you like this instead?" As he bent down to grab a hand full of sand. As the sand ran through his fingers, a thick wad of one hundred-dollar bills appeared.

"Wow! No way! I mean, yes way!" I shouted at the miraculous sight of cash appearing.

He said that gold was valuable because it's eternal and will never lose value the way paper money does. He prefers gold over paper because its properties are pure.

◆ ◆ ◆

It's More Than We Currently Understand

As I pondered the opulent significance of this moment, I couldn't help but wonder why the money and gold appearing in front of me came so effortlessly. I couldn't shake it. My mind was reeling, 'Why haven't I been able to receive it like this before without sweat and stress attached?' If I were to tell you this question didn't bother me, I would be lying to you. As I weighed in on the wad of cash now sitting in my hand, I noticed Jesus smiling at me as though he understood exactly what I was going through in the moment. I knew then he had something more to show me about my own heart.

You see, it's never about what we think we understand. It's always about what we see and believe through the eyes of oneness with Him. Whether we are aware of it or not, we are in fact one with him. It has always been his desire that we would be one in mind and spirit with him. We are made in his image and our spirit came straight out of Heaven the moment we were formed. Our inner being remembers our relationship with him up until the time we lose innocence and start taking control of our own humanity. This is when we become clouded through trauma, indoctrination, conditioning, and disappointment. However, because our spirit comes from him, he begins to give us hints of remembrance throughout our journey in life. His goodness reminds us through "epiphany moments" along the way.

What was so amazing to me about this encounter with love himself, was that he was so lighthearted, jovial, joyful, and genuinely excited about giving me provision while I was having fun with him. Especially, in one of my favorite places in the entire world. This surprised me some because I had never met anyone who got this excited about dispensing money and provision that wasn't in their physical possession all the time, yet they could have it by faith whenever they "needed" it.

◆ ◆ ◆

The Tree Of Life

Jesus knew my frustration of not seeing it manifested the way I wanted it in my own life all these years. Yet he was excited about seeing me receive the download of revelation that would cause me to experience it on a regular basis. He was watching the confusion swirling around in my brain trying to figure all of this out. So he walked over and put his arm around my shoulders to comfort and reassure me that everything was going to be more than fine. We stood there for a moment as he squeezed unbelief out of my busy mind with his presence. He said, "You know, money does grow on trees. In fact, it's a plentiful fruit hanging on the Tree of Life. It's there in every season and its eternally producing. You will never find the Tree of Life running out of its fruit of abundance."

"Huh? Please explain more! Money growing on trees?" I blurted with perplexity.

Jesus responded, "I know you want more answers, and you will certainly experience more as we walk further down the beach. Let me ask you. What are you feeling right now?"

"I feel wonderful! You are here! How could I feel anything else but that?" I said with pure elation.

"Great! So do I. We feel wonderful together because we are both partaking from the Tree of Life in this very moment. I am in you and you are in me. Love is the Tree of Life that keeps on giving out life because it is. The center of love is the fullness of life, and where love is in its fullness, non-resistance is present because we are joyfully relaxed in the present. And where the fullness of joy is, abundance is always found. In other words, there is no lack of any good thing when oneness with love and life are the center of one's focus and lifestyle.

Money growing on trees isn't an object of idolatry or desperate need when someone is feeling wonderful intertwined with the Tree of Life. And when they're feeling wonderful, non-resistance is present. When non-resistance is present, fruit simply falls off trees because its ripe for the "picking". On the contrary, fruit is hard to pick and bitter to eat when it's met with forceful resistance through effort and negative emotion. But when a person has eyes to see and a posture to receive through a sustained joy, then fruit simply falls into their experience when they remain aligned with its non-resistant nature.

That is what my nature is always like. I am the Tree of Life my friend, and you are one with me. So, the issue isn't whether or not I am willing to give you provision. It's a matter of when you are able to see it hanging on the limbs of non-resistance, and then become the joyful receiver in order to effortlessly "pluck" it out of thin air like I just did. Love is effortless and when you become aware of how you carry your emotional world, that is when all kinds of miraculous things begin to show up around you…effortlessly.

Have you ever wondered why I planted so many trees, including the Tree of Life (myself) along with a myriad of gold surrounding the Garden of Eden? It's because man was made of the same substance. He was a match to all good things around him because he lived in the flow of ease. But once he chose to leave effortless provision, he introduced effort. The kind of effort that turned into hard work. Before he decided to exchange ease for difficulty, whenever he needed sustenance he simply reached up into the tree and plucked the fruit he wanted in the moment. Work was never in the equation. Since when do you work for something that is always present and freely given?" Jesus said as he squeezed me a little tighter as we walked down the coastline together.

◆ ◆ ◆

Is Money Really The Root Of All Evil?

The warmth of the sun on my skin and the warmth of his embrace was pure bliss. My mind went from full blown frustration to calming peace with the wisdom he shared. The kind of wisdom I had been waiting to hear my whole life regarding provision and money. Now I can hear someone saying, Yeah John, that's nice, but you know that money doesn't make the world go round and having lots of it can destroy you. Why would Jesus want us to have that kind of money? Doesn't the Bible teach that money is the root of all evil? I hear you, and I have thought the very same things myself over the years, but the difference is in the choice. We can either live in fear of what money could do to us or we can simply use it as a source of blessing to all those around us.

A large portion of the Church world has done a really good job attacking wealth and placing it in the same category as evil, without ever experiencing the smile on Christ's face when he shares his thoughts about money with them. Once a person encounters his joyful presence sitting on their favorite beach laughing their heads off together, they would never exchange a wad of cash or a million gold bars for that kind of relationship...not in a gazillion years. But that's not really the point here. The relationship most definitely trumps the gold bar situation, but the gold is simply a manifestation of a surrender to his goodness without resistance attached. Besides, we are already a match to gold because it is literally found in the make-up of our own bodies in the form of minerals. Once we become receptive and non-resistant in our thought life and remain there, we attract more of it into our experience. Like begets like.

◆ ◆ ◆

Resistance Defined

Resistance is simply another way of saying, "I don't know anything else but survival. Having to fend for myself is what brought me to negative emotion and full blown resistance. So, because of that, I am going to remain fixated on worrying how I will be taken care of every moment of the day. I'm going to sit right here and put up a wall of resistance through fear so that Gods blessings can't find their way in. Smile? What smile? I haven't smiled since before I started getting into major debt. So, the only way out for me is HARD work. Why would Jesus smile on me anyways? I don't deserve to be treated well! I am a loser and a sinner anyhow! I don't feel worthy to receive something like that!"

You see, my friend, there's the resistance that keeps active faith from flowing effortlessly into our receiving mode and then there's non-resistance that keeps the walls down so things can flow into our experience without effort or hindrance. Our only "job" if you will, is to keep our gaze upon that blissful smile so that joy remains our strength to pull in what has already been provided in the unseen realm. Joy is the magnet to pull the gold of life into our realm whenever we need provision. And what is that provision? Oh man! Is it ever mind blowing! In the smallest and most profound of ways. Receiving provision isn't hard work. No, it's the complete opposite. Resistance is hard work. Handed down tradition is hard work and believing that hard work is the only way to get provision is hard work. Just think of resistance as having a bad attitude. When our attitude is bad our emotions are negative, and when they're negative, they introduce resistance that can build up like a prison wall surrounding our lives to keep provision out. *(Just think of the disciples in prison. It wasn't their unbelief through a bad attitude that flung the prison doors open. No, it was the power of joyful non-resistance that caused a quantum earthquake to happen).*

When we trust love himself through experiencing his smile every day, there no longer remains a wall of resistance or formula to be created. God pulsates with desire to give something freely. He is just simply looking for someone to laugh with as he takes care of everything else. It doesn't mean we just sit around all day eating cake and watching superhero or feel-good movies. What it does mean is when we absorb his smile each and every day, we become limitless in non-resistant creativity. And when we become creative through the peace that surpasses all understanding, we exchange hard work for effortless flow.

What Jesus was conveying to me in this moment was how faith actually works. The "Faith is the SUBSTANCE of things hoped for and the EVIDENCE of things not yet seen" kind of faith. I was tangibly aware of this lesson in the moment. It was so real and seemed so easy, yet my thoughts were still making me think it had to be hard or difficult due to my religiously trained and shame filled mind. He was saying that if I would just take time to hang out with him inwardly all throughout the day as one of his best friends conversing, laughing, and being light-hearted about things without resistance, then whenever I needed provision, all I had to do was remain childlike and receive. It's an effortless relational "exchange" that is more of an overtaking through receiving more than it is a taking. The taking part represents effort because I have to actually do something in my own self effort in order to receive something good.

Relational love is not about "doing" anything. It's about being, flowing, and receiving in the moment. It is joyful, effortless activity. This is why living in the present moment is so important to him. He lives right here not over there. The place called "there" is what we find our minds living in much of the time. It seems that many of us are always trying to get to a better season or place in life. We dwell on thoughts that bind and beat us up much of the time. Those particular thoughts take us out of the present now and keep us living in either the past or a "better" life in the future.

◆ ◆ ◆

No Such Thing As A Place Called "There"

We say things like, "When I move over there or when I get my business going, or when I get that pay increase, or when I find the right person for me, or when I get that book written, or when my kids go off to college, or when I make enough money some-day I will live on Maui." The problem with a place called "there" is that we take our minds there and we leave the "here" place where Jesus resides! We take our thoughts with us to the past failures, inadequacies, hurts, and regrets. We dwell on how we think God operates based upon what we've learned through childhood trauma, and religious conditioning. We sometimes feel abandoned because of some past event, so we think we have to make something happen on our own, without realizing his smile has already taken care of it all.

This was a moment with Christ I knew I had to cherish, because this very situation is the manifestation of what he has been speaking to me about for a long time.

When Jesus finished pitching the wad of hundred-dollar bills back into the spirit realm, we continued to walk further down the beach having fun discussing his life intertwined with mine. I knew in my heart the reason he threw the money back through the veil was because I didn't have a need for the cash in this very moment. In other words, I didn't have a want or a need for that kind of cash while I was fellowshipping with the one who owns it all to begin with. Where would I deposit the money anyway? What would I spend it on while walking with Jesus on the beach? If I simply slipped it into my pocket to spend later, then it would become a distraction from keeping me present with the love of my life. It would have the potential of becoming my security blanket for a while and blurring the innocence of faith from re-maining one with Christ and receiving his goodness in the mo-ment. *(I mean, it's not like he couldn't just simply pop another wad of cash or gold bar out of thin air later on if he wanted to, right? He's God!)*

◆ ◆ ◆

The Divine Dance Of Oneness

As I thought about all of this glorious goodness, he turned to me and said, "Do you want to see how this oneness thing works?" "Well, yes! I Sure do!" I said with great excitement. He then bumped His right shoulder into mine and vanished into me. He "absorbed or translated" into me and became one with my very being. It was so surreal. If I could try to describe to you what it looked like when he became one with me, is like one of the crew members on the Star Trek ship being beamed somewhere inside the teleportation machine. It's like he was being pixelized as he transitioned. As he did, I felt this surge of love and power come into me like I've never felt before. I felt a rush that would make your insides burst with power and love. It was supernaturally super-charged, yet it felt so naturally familiar. Like we had been one all along from the beginning of time. It was awesome to say the least!

Then, just as quickly as he entered my being, he popped out the other side, walked in front of me, and stopped. He looked straight into my eyes, and said, "Watch this!". All of the sudden the Father and Holy Spirit showed up and joined him in a circle around me. I was utterly stunned, but in a really good way. In fact, I started laughing with overwhelming joy because I felt so at home with the experience watching the Trinity surround me. As they began to fully reveal themselves, they too began to walk through my being one by one circling through me several times until we all broke out into a dance. It was a relational dance that no one really understands until they've entered into it too. It's indescribable. It's ecstatic joy and full acceptance. It's exhilarating and breath taking all at the same time, because you know that you know, you belong to them and nothing can take you out of their hands. They are all powerful and fully intimate in knowing every part of you. They are three in one yet three to one. They are the fun expression of love and they make you feel as if you've never sinned a day in your life. There's no need or want in their presence except to remain. When you become one with their eternal dance of unconditional love, there's no amount of cash, gold, or rare gemstone that could ever replace it.

I was undone. I was standing on a beach that I love in the presence of a God I love even more, completely satisfied. I now entered into a knowing that provision wasn't something I had to work for, beg for, strive for, or even quote all the right scriptures for. It was all because they are the very definition of love... period.

As the dance subsided, my body felt like it had been through the best spa-like treatment on the planet. Father, Jesus, and Holy Spirit all stood there looking into one another with a depth of adoration that just couldn't be explained. I watched as Jesus stared into his Father's eyes with such profound love, that it made you cry uncontrollably at the thought of what it meant to them and humanity. Holy Spirit was standing next to them with a nurturing presence that was so overwhelmingly thick in the air you could cut it with a knife. To say it was an honor to behold this moment was a gross understatement. It was if I had died and went to Heaven witnessing what constantly happens inside the throne room and beyond.

While I stood there paralyzed by this unexplainable love, Jesus turned towards me and said, "How was that? Did you like the dance?". "Uh, uh, umm" I was speechless, and he knew it. My knees buckled and I hit the sand like a dead man. I bawled by eyes out with gratitude and appreciation. I don't know how long I was there, but I didn't care. I couldn't help it. My entire being was overwhelmed by this amazing love. After what seemed like a while, I felt a loving hand touch the top of my head, followed by a gentle kiss touching my forehead. I looked up and saw Jesus smiling as he reached out his hand to help me up off of the warm sand. As strength began to enter back into my legs to stand, neither of us said a word as we started walking down the beach together. It was one of those moments where no words were needed, because presence said it all.

"When you've spent time in the presence of someone who is fully present consumed with the fullness of love, few words are needed to have the conversation of a lifetime."

◆ ◆ ◆

My Sack Full Of Effort

We walked a little further and then suddenly came to a stop. Something caught my attention from behind us. It was an awareness that caused me to stop. We both turned around to look to see what I was feeling. My mouth dropped open at the site. What I saw was me walking with what looked like a gigantic sack tied around my neck and shoulders, bouncing high above my head. I was walking down the beach towards us. I stood there speechless that I could see another me! Jesus saw the shocked looked on my face and said, "What you are seeing is the old you walking towards the new you. All things were made new before you were even you. Oh yes, this is gonna be awesome!" I looked over at him and sheepishly whispered, "Boy I hope so!". As I looked on, strangely, I knew what was inside the sack I was carrying before I physically saw what was inside. They were "things", my things. The bag was crammed full of them. The sack sort of looked like that huge, red bag of stolen Christmas gifts the Grinch had on top of the mountain in the movie, *"The Grinch who Stole Christmas"*. Only it wasn't as ominous looking to me as I walked towards us standing on the beach. Somehow, I just knew those things stuffed in the bag represented all of my own efforts.

I stood there next to Jesus watching me bounce down the beach kind of proud of my own accomplishments gained through sweat and toil. It wasn't like those "things" were all evil. Some were in fact, good.

Upon seeing the bag, Jesus wasn't fazed at all or taken back in the slightest. It was as if he was thinking, "Good job John! You did well for yourself. Now how does it make you feel?" I then turned to him and egoically thought to myself, "Actually, it feels kinda good! Look at what I gained through the gifts, talents, and abilities you gave me! I did it all for you!" He looked at me lovingly, paused for a moment, then did something I had no way of being prepared for. He walked over towards the water, reached up into the sky and grabbed hold of something that was invisible to my eyes.

◆ ◆ ◆

The Doorway Of Opulence

"Flash!"

A blinding light hit the sand. To my shock, a huge, shimmering, gold-colored curtain standing higher than the natural eye could see suddenly appeared in front of us on the beach. Jesus had a hold of the edge of it. With a big smile on his face he said, "Thank you my friend for all of your efforting, but take a look at this!" He then yanked open the curtain. As the curtain swung open, I couldn't believe my eyes. I was in shock, to say the least. The site of it took my breath away, literally. I fell backwards in the sand in awe. What I beheld was so magnificent, words could not describe what I was seeing. I gasped for air as the blinding radiance of Heavens opulence hit me, and the glory of it was exploding through every cell of my being. It was sheer beauty, wealth, and abundance, like I had never seen before or imagined in my wildest dreams. It was beyond imagining. It was utterly spectacular. So much so that it completely drained my strength. It felt like all of the blood drained from my body in a split second. All I could do was lean into the safety and strength I felt when I was walking with Jesus down the beach a few seconds ago. It was like the awe of Gods splendor just opened up to a grey, colorless world and made the darkness of my own understanding bow its knee, whether it wanted to or not. It was like all of Heaven opened up before the earth and I hadn't a clue of what to do.

While I lay there paralyzed in the tangibility of who Christ was, and the wealth of Heaven exploding in front of me, all of my own efforts became mere space-dust before the entire cosmos. That bag I was carrying around my shoulders chocked of accomplishments? Yeah, well, with one pull on Heaven's curtain...my bag of effort became like a millstone of burden around my entire life in a hot second.

My mind went there for a moment, but then my attention quickly came back to the wonder and power of what I was beholding. As far up as I could see there was a translucent, solid-gold wall, filled with shining jewels of every kind imaginable, and some I had never seen before. The glistening from the gems in the wall was so profoundly bright that it lit up not only the beach, but the islands, and the entire world. It's as if a million ton "nuclear" atomic device just went off, only brighter.

All I could muster up in the little strength I had left in my voice was, "Wow! Wow! Wow!". I was gasping for air in light of this heavenly oxygenated substance hitting my body.

◆ ◆ ◆

A Diamond From Heaven

As I lay there in shock on the hot sand *(the heat radiating from the glistening wall was so intense that it heated the sand to a temperature that felt like I was sitting in a hot tub)* I heard an incredibly thunderous sound likened unto a heavy hail shower come down and slap the beach in front of me. It was so loud that it caused the sand to shiver violently all around. Wave after wave of thunderous movement surrounded my feet. My heart began to race with the thoughts of the unknown.

"Wack!!!!" "Boom!" another loud smack hit the sand.

I looked up and couldn't believe my eyes! Before me standing twenty or more feet out of the sand I saw a 'dinosauric' sized, perfectly cut, diamond. It hit the sand so hard that it drove the tip down to about waist deep. The gemstone was as big as a train car and probably weighed just as much. The glistening and shine coming off of it was blindingly beautiful. The radiant light from the wall shined directly onto the diamond, causing its many facets to cascade rainbow colors all over the islands and the skies above. It seemed like the colors were beyond 5K. They were otherworldly.

After I attempted to clear my eyes from the brightness, I turned to my right and saw Jesus run over to the diamond, jump up on top of it and say, "It's all here and it's all yours! Do you like it?" "Uh, Umm, Uh", I sat there speechless in complete amazement and wonder of what was taking place in front of me. How could I answer? The words weren't there. I was truly speechless! This was too overwhelming for me! I couldn't describe what I was seeing and feeling. I was struck numb by the power of his presence and the provision he was revealing.

While I was sitting there speechless with my jaw in the sand, I watched Jesus jump from gemstone to gemstone as they crashed into the sand one by one from the top of the cascading wall of opulence. This is where my mind started going even more crazy with thoughts from my own bag of futile efforts and the things I learned over the years in religion. My mind kept racing back and forth between, "Is that really Jesus telling me this kind of wealth is all mine? No way! I was taught in religion this kind of opulence would destroy me! Money is "THE" root of all evil, right?" But at the same time my entire inner being was shouting, "Yes! Yes! Yes! This isn't the "devil" jumping from jewel to jewel in front of me! This is God Himself showing me all of this!"

Man, what a mental war in the moment. I was literally getting a "crash" course on what Jesus thinks of wealth and it was mentally overwhelming. It's not like I've spent my life begging for money or striving to make money my main goal or anything. I knew he wasn't showing me this as some kind of lesson about the importance of keeping away from wealth. That was evident in the way I felt when I saw the smile on his face when he tossed me the first gold bar. All this experience was doing was making me want to be closer to him.

"People have issues with idolatry surrounding money when they don't understand what it means to God from a heavenly perspective. Idols become idols when people live in separation from him through their own survival, believing they won't be taken care of through surrender."

ENTER THE HEART OF HUMANITY

After crashing my mind for a while, Jesus stopped on top of one of the giant gemstones in front of a huge opening that now appeared in the center of the wall that was behind the curtain. It sort of looked like one of those grand, circle-shaped archways that you would see in a castle or historic building in Europe somewhere. Although, the difference in this one was every square inch was covered in a wide array of silver, gold, and precious gemstones that took your breath away. What was even more interesting to me was the archway opening felt alive and familiar. It was like it was a part of me. The archway opening led to an inside world of some kind, and I wanted to know what was in it. It's like I couldn't help but want to explore more of what felt like a part of me.

As I looked on in wonder, I heard Jesus say, "Come! Let's go inside. I have many things to show you!". Little did I know at the time, but he was taking me straight into the core of my own heart and the heart of humanity. I was about to embark on the spiritual journey of a lifetime. One that would change the landscape of my thinking, forever. The spirit realm is filled with unlimited possibility and this was one of those seemingly 'impossibly' possible moments I just had to know more about.

As we walked through the archway, I noticed the walls and ceiling were pulsating with life. They were beating like the sound of a massive heart. This is where things began to get more serious. I could tell not only by the Lords' posture as we began to enter into the corridor of the main artery, but by the look and feel inside. I noticed something different about it. The light that was so blinding on the outside, began to fade a little when we moved underneath the archway to enter. There was also something on the ceiling of the hallway just beyond the main entrance that looked light a large shadow.

The beating sound got louder and louder as we made our way in. It sounded like I just walked into the heart of the beginning and ending of the entire human race. It was that enormous. The beating sound was awesome yet sobering at the same time. I didn't know what to make of it really. I just knew that Jesus was my rock and the safety I needed as he was about to show me something beyond my own limited understanding.

The Load We Were Never Meant to Carry

As we made our way further into the opening of this wondrous "temple", I noticed Jesus pick something up and he was getting ready to throw it towards the ocean as the waves lapped up against his legs. *(I kept thinking that even though this enormous archway had appeared there, the really intriguing part to me was the fact we were still walking in sand along the shore in the natural realm as well. It was two worlds colliding into one.)*

Naturally, my curiosity to see what Jesus was holding drew me closer to him. As I got to where he was standing, I could see he was holding a little crab in his hand. To my surprise, he was prying a gemstone out of its left claw as he was swinging it towards the water. I thought, "That's odd? I wonder why he would care about a crab walking around with a gemstone in its claw?" As I pondered this a little more, I noticed that he picked up another crab and then another, as he took gemstones out of their claws. I wondered why he was so adamant about taking the jewels away from them. Then, I saw it. The crabs were trying to run away with some of the precious gemstones that were blazing their glorious splendor all over the beach.

Hmmm, what does this mean? I thought. But before I could even ask, Jesus answered my thoughts. He said, "It's important that I don't let these smart little critters get away with the jewels. The crabs come here to try and steal what has not been freely given to them. They think it's ok to run away with provision that belongs to humanity through their own intellect. Did you notice the gemstones are bigger than their little bodies can carry? These crabs represent the left side of your brain that are saturated with thoughts that produce striving, self-effort, future worry, and fear. They come to make your house of communion a den of distraction and stress.

You see, what these little guys do is steal precious memories and moments of our time of peace and rest together in the present. They're a distraction. They love to take what has not been appointed to them to try and use it for something else. They were born for another purpose. What are they going to do with gemstones? Build themselves a beautiful little house in the sea? Sell them to pay their bills? LOL. Jewels in the claws of crabs look out of place because they are. The crabs think they know what they're doing with them but will only lose them in the waves of an ocean pushing back.

In other words, when something like wealth has been pre sented to an animal, or in this case the intellect, it will become lost in the waves of opposition, because it is not received through non-resistance. A creature or animal doesn't have the capacity to utilize gemstones as provision because they have been freely given their own in the form of food and shelter. In the same way, the wealth you see here has been freely provided in a form that can be exchanged for the same. I give animals everything they need. Their only "work" is to gather what is already there. Gemstones are not a part of that gathering, but they are a part of yours. This is why I have hidden them in the soil of the earth since creation, but I am about to open up the cosmos in a way that will bring them to the surface for easy gathering for all who dwell in joyful non-resistant flow.

◆ ◆ ◆

No Costume Jewelry Found Here

Notice that these beautiful stones are all near the opening and embedded in the walls? I know you do my friend, and they are there for good reason. For where your heart is there is also treasure. I know you treasure mine, and that's why you don't see any rust, erosion, or cubic zirconia around yours. Your heart posture of gratitude and authenticity are where these treasures are found. Moving into heart-centeredness is where my smile is known, and effortless provision is always present. But we will discuss more on that a little later. You see, worry and toil are the outcome of striving. I want my people to know what effortless provision is through trust and play alone. There's no need to strive for something I have already given or go after something that is misaligned with your life. Adam was a picture of what life can be like when you simply have fun with me. Every source of provision was already given prior to Adam walking the earth because of wild creativity and unconditional love. I had a blast creating a world that I would want to have fun dwelling in. This is why Adam was made in my image. He knew nothing else but creative play in the beginning. Sweat was introduced only when he allowed the "crabs" to come in and steal his treasure of non-resistant play.

You see, when something shiny and beautiful appears in front of a person that is dealing with "crabby" thoughts embedded with reasoning, they will always attempt to strive for a form of provision that is entirely too much to carry. Then when they attempt to run away with it, my grace steps in to help provide a way of escape. This is why you are seeing me take the gemstones out of the claws of these little guys."

"Ok? Wow! Now that makes a lot of sense!" My mind was screaming with more questions and reeling with thoughts of my own crab-ridden mentality when it came to provision. "But what about the ones you missed? Some of the crabs got away with the jewels!" I bluntly said to Jesus.

"Nah, they haven't gotten away with anything. The waves will take care of them. Don't worry, they won't kill them, but after they tumble around in that giant washing machine a few times trying to get away with carrying that heavy load, they will wish they had dropped what was never theirs to carry. I wanted to help them, but they were just too determined to run away in their own penny "pinching", misaligned effort to even see me standing there waiting to help. The sparkle of a future provision was compelling them forward. They know better, but they try to get away with carrying the weight of it, nonetheless. It's the "crabby" nature of things". Jesus said with a sigh.

Ok, I felt that one. I could see my own life inside one of these little hard-shelled critters. I could feel my own mercy starting to extend more towards every "crab" on the planet. Where before I never wanted to get that close to one because of their painful claws and scary little faces.

◆ ◆ ◆

The Karoshi Stance

Jesus was simply and profoundly showing me what my own effort was doing to my life. Sure, we can go and sweat it out busting our back in misalignment trying to bring in provision for ourselves, but at what cost? The price is way too high! It's no wonder something looked completely off when I watched the tiny little crabs try to carry giant gemstones in their claws. I don't know why my mind went there, but it made me think of the Japanese term called "Karoshi" which means death by overwork and exhaustion. People literally drop dead from overworking themselves trying to carry something that was never meant to be carried. Working for a better tomorrow while missing the beautiful provision and grace of today is costly. Oh yes, it may very well look and sound honorable to work hard, but when it's misaligned, it has the potential of throwing everything else out of alignment; including lower backs, kidneys, families, governments, and total dysfunction in society.

I kept thinking this is why I have been so stressed out focusing on the paycheck trying to chase something down to gain enough provision to take care of the bills that were due NEXT month! When all along I could have just remained in restful union in the now with provision himself creating wonderful things that are in alignment with who I am today. There's no effort involved with that. Since when does fun include effort? The good things in life, the hobbies, the play, the melting of dark chocolate on the tongue, the enjoyment of creating with your hands, and the hilarious fun of laughing your head off with close friends. We experience joy in spurts along our journey when it should be the daily norm. We shouldn't feel guilty when we laugh our brains out over something that is indeed funny. Where did we get laughter from anyways? Could it be because God himself laughs? Of course, He does! He created it because he knew humanity would need its healthy, untainted medicine.

It became obvious to me that is why he told His people through his disciple Paul to think on things that are pure, lovely, true, and good. He was telling us to guard our hearts from things that would take us away from joy because the issues of life and how we see them flow from the heart. I suddenly knew why he said the heart without fellowship with him is desperate and lost, because, like these little crabs, they take things that are priceless and time that is valuable.

I could tell my thoughts were somewhat humorous to The Lord because He was smiling at me as he gently flung another crab into the deep-blue ocean. His care was revealed even more in making sure some of them made it over the crashing waves and into the deep, where they could at least ride one of the waves back onto shore, instead of being crushed by them.

I've learned that our choices do have consequences. We can choose to be stubborn and head straight into a crashing force that could harm us, or we can simply remain surrendered to present alignment with the love of the one who effortlessly provides. Watching Jesus remove the gemstones out of the claws of the crabs with such care reminded me that alignment with his compassion is where provision is abundant. I knew he was, is, and always will be the only way to a life of abundant well-being.

Jesus playfully interjected my thoughts saying, "Right this way my friend, follow me further into the heart!"

◆ ◆ ◆

Love Does Not Set Out To Embarrass

As I walked closely behind him, he stopped suddenly, smiled, and said, "Let's walk together, side by side. Don't be concerned, I'm not going to embarrass you. After all, this is the entryway into the heart of everyone. It won't be as bad as you think. I've already taken care of it. I just want you to see how much I love you and desire the best for your life".

I thought to myself, "Ok! What a relief! I was having such a wonderful time up until now thinking I was going to be exposed on a whole new level."

Seeing my relief, Jesus said, "Oh! by the way, all of these gem-stones, silver, gold, and other valuable treasures that you see here? Yeah, that is how I see the heart of what I created in you! I'm not looking to expose you. I am merely exposing you to the treasures of your own heart." (I think my face just melted off my body. By now I could hardly function. I was thinking to myself... 'I'm good now'. Let me float on into Heaven. I'm really quite satisfied with what you just said Jesus).

He continued, "Friend, do you remember what I said about the Garden of Eden in the book of Genesis?"
"Yes, what part?" I answered.
He said, "The part about all of the gold surrounding the "Aorta" of the Garden itself?"

"Yes, I think so, ok?" I responded.

"Well, my friend, the Garden represents living in the atmosphere of union with me. You see, after Adam decided to walk away from my care and provision, it cast a shadow of doubt upon my ability to fully provide for him without him ever having to sweat for it. It wasn't my choice to pull back from providing every-thing he needed in the moment. It was his. He was blinded by indecision of what he thought his future was like. It was called "doublemindedness", in modern terms. Adam took himself out of the present with me to stand in the future of the valley of decision trying to decide which way to go. I had given him free will to have the freedom to make a choice in the present now.

That shadow you saw along the ceiling of this entry is just that... choice. Choice based upon a perceived future outcome. Man chooses to live in question of my provision, because it doesn't reveal itself in the timing or the way he wants it to. And when he does question, fear blinds the beauty of what is always here.

You see, I have never taken away opulence from humanity. No, man believes that because of choice. He decides to strive and sweat for what has always been here through trusting the now with joy. The gold surrounding the Garden represents creativity flowing through the arteries of the heart. I created Eden as an example to reveal what the heart looks like when it is at rest and flooded with joy. Provision naturally flows in and around a life that is playfully engaged in love. This is all for you my friend, I'm giving you a brighter perspective. I've taken care of the shadows once and for all. I've just dimmed the lights in here a bit to show you where you've been. You've now crossed over into trust and I appreciate how you let me handle the "crabby" mentality that was trying to steal from you." Jesus said with a laugh.

Stunned, I did what any intelligent person would do at this point...I kept quiet and listened as love began to walk me through the heart of my own humanity. I never really understood what it meant to pull back from the heart and hand of his provision by living in the future or the past until now. I could feel the depth of care Jesus was conveying while He shared. I began to see where decision and choice based upon the illusion of a perceived outcome could lead me down the road of worry, fear, pain, and unnecessary suffering.

The good news is I didn't feel one ounce of condemnation or disappointment coming from his countenance or his words. Just the fullness of love and care. It was absolutely amazing to me because I had always felt condemnation coming from myself and others when I tried to share about mistakes or "wrong" choices I made that led to more pain. I mean, it's bad enough when you make a decision that turns out to be egoically painful, but then to have "well-meaning" people try to tell you how stupid you were for making it? Yeah, that's a tough one for sure.

There's that smirk again.

I knew He knew what I was thinking. Jesus turned and looked over to the right as if to say, "Walk this way, I want to show you more."

◆ ◆ ◆

The Writing On The Wall

"Look! Over there!" He said as he pointed to the walls of the main corridor. "There's the writing on the wall! Can you see it?" I could see the writing, but I couldn't make out what it said. It wasn't written in English. I squinted my eyes to try and interpret the writing and noticed how the walls themselves were stunning with what looked to be like shimmering gold "veins" running through them. The only difference was they didn't quite follow through and connect with each other the way human veins would do. I continued to ponder what these words on the wall said and what the gold "veins" represented.
Sure enough, Jesus knew what I was thinking and said, "The written words say, "Mysterious adventure awaits all who enter the Artery of Trust".

He continued, "It's a mystery to me why people would simply choose not to trust in the adventure of my goodness over their own painful pursuits. That is why you see the broken veins leading to the chamber of trust. People think they have to toil and stress overworking to meet their own needs through knowledge. What you see are broken neuropathways inside the Tree of Knowledge mentality. They are broken because the nourishment of life is missing. Hard work and stress have become their brokenness. If people only knew that it's much easier than what their beliefs first told them to be about provision.

You see my friend, broken families and religious conditioning do a good job of raising people in worry, so they gain knowledge to think up formulas and strategies that match their survival mentalities to get their needs met. Formulas just don't work when it comes to mystery, the mystery of trust. It's not a complicated mystery though. It just simply means that I want to surprise my friends with the best, and that my friend, is a mystery some do not want. It's too easy and unfamiliar. It takes the element of control out of it, and I never control anyone. I just want to be with them enjoying our time together so they can see I can be trusted to provide through the 'mystery' of love, and care.

Humanity is prone to predictability instead of living in the mystery of the great unknown. And the unknown is where knowledge ends, and trust begins inside the Tree of Life. I didn't create trust as something that can be obtained through knowledge alone. Trust is the adventure of living in the glorious wonder of love, fully satisfied in me. I am love and I can be completely trusted."

I couldn't help but grab my head in the moment as I heard these life-giving words rivet through my own unbelief. It's one thing to be hard on yourself because you somehow feel like you let God down through fear and disbelief. It's another to stand before the very heart of my own humanity with the words, "Mysterious adventure awaits all who enter the Artery of Trust" written on them, and grieve because trust is all you ever wanted to do since you began your walk with Love Himself. It felt like my very own heart couldn't add up to what was being shown to me in the moment, and it was hard to express the level of grief I felt. It's like He was allowing me to feel the weight of doubt inside the heart of the entire human race as I stood there. It wasn't like He was doing it to me, it was the emotional draining of what striving and self-effort felt like inside the soul of man after attempting to trust God millions of times over through their own efforted intellect.

I thought, 'this is me too!' How many times have I tried to have faith in my own strength and then call it God? How many attempts have I made at living an adventurous "faith" filled life only to find out much of it was mere presumption fueled by ego? How many scripture verses and declarations have I made just to try and get God to hear my plea for money? These things kept racing through my mind as I heard and felt the voice of humanity trying to please a God who isn't demanding it.

As I stood there pondering the gravity of my ten- thousand-pound efforted attempts at formula creating, I began to let go of my trained understanding that was crushing me with frustration. Why wouldn't God, the God who is love, want to provide for me without any strings of effort attached? I have often said that my wife and children would never need to do anything for me in order to provide everything that was good for them. It's only when I've allowed my ego to dominate the picture is when I've withheld something to serve my own fears in some way. God doesn't play like that. He doesn't have an egoic nature. He is pure, unadulterated love, with nothing to prove through self-preservation. We've just been taught that we need to do something for him in order to receive something back.

My mind was racing with all the scripture verses I had ever heard and even preached over the years about transactionary provision. And the belief that I needed to put on some kind of dog and pony show in order for God to bless me. I guess the weight of that grief and frustration must have shown because Jesus didn't say a word to address those things in the moment. He just kept looking at me with a gentleness, and joy that was louder than the heartbeat of humanity I was entering.

"Just you wait!" Jesus said excitedly. "Wait until you see all the majesty on the inside of this artery! You are going to be blown away my friend! This is going to be so good!"

He was giddy with excitement, smiling and laughing like a child in an enormous candy store just waiting to dive in. He couldn't wait to show me what trust looked like from the inside out. Perhaps it would trump the feeling I had when He told me about the broken veins. I kept thinking about what that meant. Why would he continue to show me my own doubt-filled heart knowing how I feel right now? Yeah, well, like I said before, just keep quiet and listen, right? I was used to living in and out of a survival mentality and my mind was having a hard time absorbing the freedom of effortless trust. The good thing is I still hadn't once felt any shame coming from him that would make me feel like joining the crabs in the ocean to beat myself up some more.

"Walk this way!" Jesus said jokingly as he attempted to walk like a crab towards the entrance of the Trust Artery.

I broke out laughing seeing the Creator of the Universe act like a child in front of me. Oh, how refreshingly relieving that was to see. One thing I know about Jesus is that he has the greatest sense of humor, doesn't He? I'm beginning to understand that he is more like us than we first thought.

As I meditated on these things, I couldn't help but be distracted by the loud "thumping" noise that continued to rivet throughout the entrance and into the tunnel of the artery. "So, Jesus, what is that thumping noise I keep hearing? It's so loud!" I said bluntly.

◆ ◆ ◆

The Rhythm Of The Heart Knows

He turned, smiled, and said, "Oh that? Yeah, that's your heart pounding. I'm allowing you to hear your own heart in the midst of humanity".

I responded with somewhat of a surprise, "My heart is doing that? It sounds like I'm running or something! It's beating so fast!"

Jesus continued, "It's pumping fast because that is the sound of fear, worry, stress, and self-effort. I'm taking you through the inside of the Artery of Trust to show you the volume level of not only your own heart, but the heart of humanity as a whole. I want you to hear what I hear each and every moment of the day. Notice how the sound causes a vibration that is felt? That's because we are traveling through the corridor of a main artery. That sound travels through the rest of the body and eventually makes it's way out through the tissue walls and into the atmosphere surrounding the body. That, my friend, is called frequency. More on that later. But for now, don't worry, the noise level will begin to subside as we travel further in." He turned and waved me forward.

"Oh! Wow! Ok!" I said with wonder as I followed him in.

You know what was so amazing to me about the words he just spoke? Every time he said something the loud thumping sound subsided a little. His words made my heart calm; like peace flooding my entire being causing my heart to rest.

Have you ever had your heart slow down to the point where it startled you enough to make you start checking your pulse in a panic? Yeah, me too! This was definitely one of those times. In fact, I'm quite sure it was a little humorous to the Lord because I kept checking my wrist for a pulse while he was talking. I'm starting to believe there's so much more to the physical and spiritual heart connection than we could have ever comprehended. *(All I can tell you is that even as I am writing this my heart is at rest. Of course, I'm not checking my pulse every five seconds, but I think you get the picture. I pray you feel the same sense of rest as you "selah" through this encounter with me.)*

Every step I take further into the artery I can feel my mind, soul, and body healing from my own toil-filled efforts.

CHAMBER 1

Enter the Artery of Trust

"Now, when we enter, watch your head!" Jesus exclaimed.

"Wow! What is this? Why is the opening of the artery so small?" I said with perplexity. "It's not that it's small my friend, this is just an area where anxiety has caused a constriction in the opening." Jesus answered.

"A constriction?" I asked.

Jesus continued, "Yes, like a natural human artery would do when there's a blockage. What you are seeing is the effects of fear and doubt trying to close off the maturity of belief. And if it isn't dealt with then eventually this part of the artery will close, causing a backup to occur. Once that happens, then trust turns into a panic attack. Once panic takes hold then fear attacks. Once fear rushes in, now it's a set up for a stroke. You see my friend; a stroke is an outward sign of a heart that is void of essential nutrients found in fresh food, and the spiritual nutrients found in trust.

People don't have to experience the amount of pain they do in certain areas of life if trust is present to keep the artery clear of constriction. It's impossible to live in mature trust and have a constriction in flow, the flow of provision. And that flow is as effortless as an unobstructed artery is carrying blood to all parts of the body. A person doesn't pay attention to their own heart pumping blood as they go about their day. It's the same way with provision flowing through unobstructed trust.

Ok! Are you ready? Let's do this! No need to hold your breath, just walk in after me through the wall of liquid." Jesus exclaimed with joy.

"Ok? Wall of liquid?" I asked with trepidation.

"Oh, yes, that's just oxygenated blood that flows through the artery. We will be walking downstream, so don't worry about breathing hard or running out of air. Once we enter it's all smooth sailing from here." He said with glee.

"But we are walking into liquid blood, how will I even breathe?" I exclaimed with reservation.

"No need to fear, I am your oxygen inside the blood. Picture this kind of like you would imagine the inside of your mother's womb to be, only better. Just follow close behind me and you'll be consumed by my oxygen as we walk through the artery. You know what it's like to breathe underwater, you've been scuba diving before, it's similar to that!" He said with excitement.

"But that's different! I had a regulator in my mouth and oxygen was coming through the hose!" I shouted.

"Why is that any different? My breath is in you and my presence is with you. Just act like I'm your regulator and the hose is connected to the tank of my presence...sort of like an umbilical cord is to a baby. Just breathe in and out slowly. You'll hear my heartbeat as we walk through the artery. It's all through trust that I will keep you safe. Ready?" He said with assurance.

"Uh, Ok! Yes, ok! I got this! Just breathe in and breathe out John. Yes, I got this!" I sheepishly said with anxiety in my tone.

I walked closely behind him as we moved into the pulsating chamber of trust.

Whoosh! Gasp!

I could hear and feel the rush of oxygen hit my lungs like a mighty wind. Holy oxygen exploded in my chest and it felt like every cell in my body came to life as I drew a breath. It felt like I was getting a total cleanse, only this kind of cleanse felt like complete rejuvenation. "Wow! This is amazing! Could this be what it means to be fully alive? Is this what it feels like to breathe "under water?" I was feeling an invincibility I had never known before. My mind raced back to what he said about being like a baby in a mothers' womb. Is this what the fullness of innocence is like? I felt so clean and whole. I kept breathing in and out just so I could feel the power of this kind of purity. Breath by breath, step by step, I followed him further into the artery.

As I looked ahead, I began to notice something about the way he walked. He wasn't walking persay, he was actually bouncing with every step. It was like he was checking the "floor" of the artery or something. You know, much like you would do to test the safety of a wooden bridge or a sheet of ice on the surface of a frozen lake. It's like he was making sure it was "safe" enough to walk on. It was puzzling to me as to why he would appear to be doing that.

Sure enough, Jesus stopped and answered my thoughts, "Oh, I'm not checking to see if it's safe enough to walk on, I am bouncing because that's what you do when you know what trust feels like. It's like when you were a child having fun in a rubber bouncy playhouse, remember? You see, I never stop believing in the heart's ability to trust, because I designed it to. It's simply a matter of time before much of humanity leans completely and entirely into the bounce themselves.

Rest assured, it will happen when the stress of fear becomes too much for the heart to handle. Meaning, when the stress of self-effort comes near the center of the heart, it has no choice but to bow to complete trust once it sees the treasures awaiting its arrival. In other words, the resistance effort has produced surrenders to the beauty of effortless generosity. That is why I talk about the importance of living from a heart-centered reality.

Jesus continued...

"Love is free and effortless. There are no strings attached in the divine "bouncy" room of freedom. Think about it my friend, when you are hanging out and laughing with those you love in the natural with childlike innocence, your mind isn't thinking about how to pull some strings to get what you want. You are flowing in the moment of an effortless situation. This is the state of being that keeps you heart-centered inside the treasure that is always present.

In other words, home is where your spirit is eternally present, and because it is, provision is always there. Laughter and joy are the elements that keep it all flowing whenever it's "needed". You can't laugh and be frustrated at the same time. It's like having bitter and sweet water flowing from the same well at the same time. It's either sweet or it's bitter, but not both.

The Artery of Trust is well aware of the things that try to come

and block the flow of our close fellowship inside the center of life. That is why I have a spring in my step, because I know you are now entering the artery that leads to your spiritual living room of well-being. Many people have tried to enter and remain, but that is why you see the broken veins on the wall. The Tree of Knowledge keeps them continually efforting through guessing, and that's why it doesn't work for them. It's not a matter of "trying" to trust me for anything you have need of or desire. It's a matter of surrendering to trust in the Tree of Life with me and allowing the flow of that surrender to take you all the way in.

Another way to look at it lays in the fast food/drive-thru mentality. When you go out to order food you get specific items on the menu, and then when you don't receive them in a few minutes at the window you get frustrated through impatience. In the same way, when you ask me for anything it's already done. But everything you desire may not come in a few minutes. That is why trust and patience are so important in life.

Why? Not because I'm a cruel taskmaster forcing you to wait, but because you get to lose resistance by engaging joy until those things manifest. This keeps you in a state of receiving without resistance attached, so that whatever you want or have need of comes faster. But when you become frustrated and impatient because you are not seeing them manifest right away, you have a tendency to move back to being like the little crab straining to carry the heavy load of self-effort.

This is also where humanity thinks hard work is a noble and honorable thing to do. It may in fact seem beautiful like the gemstone, but what glory does anyone get out of gaining something that causes them to have to work even harder to get more? Why not take the easy route? Playful trust is effortless and easy. It's the patience part that people equate with hard work. What are you in a hurry for anyways? Let's enjoy our time together. I know what you need before you even ask. And because I do, all that is needed is playful trust. There's nothing "hard" about that.

Things are only hard when you think you have to bust your back to get them. That is a human thing not mine. When people tell one another, they had a "hard" day at work what they are really exuding is misalignment, and they are asking to be aligned with their own authentic flow of creativity. Trust is the beginning of effortlessness. Once a person relaxes into playful trust, that is when resistance to what you don't want is surrendered and the blessings then begin to flow.

◆ ◆ ◆

Blessings Are Always Looking For A Way In

Picture it like a sealed glass bubble or a round dome surrounding your body. This is what resistance or hard work is like. The harder you try the thicker the glass becomes around you. Yes, you can still see through it, but what do you see? All of your wants and needs standing on the outside of the glass with no way in. They are looking at you and you are looking back at them wondering why they can't get to you. They search for an opening all around the glass bubble you've created, but there's no sign of a window, door, or access point to get in. This is where your frustration level begins to reach an all-time high and then you start to complain as to why it's not working.

This is what effort looks like through worried resistance. The more you beg for things because you don't see them coming at the speed you want them to, the thicker the glass becomes, until it turns into a magnifying glass over your life. And you know what happens when the sun hits a magnifying glass and you're the target of its spotlight, don't you? Yes, you know, things begin to heat up really quickly. This can be a good thing because the discomfort then causes you to rethink some things. You start to see the contrast. Better yet, pain causes you to stop thinking altogether, and to start feeling the elation and relief of trust once you relent and give in to non-resistance."

"Wow! That was a lot! But it makes so much more sense to me now!" I exclaimed with relief.

"Why is it that we have such a challenge trusting the only one who can be fully trusted? I've always known that our thoughts are powerful, but I hadn't realized just how much they were actually contributing to the resistance that acted like a shield around me! I was taught that it had more to do with my unbelief combined with some kind of demonic force holding them back!" I sparked with a level of regret in my tone.

Jesus responded, "Well, yes, and no, my friend. Yes, your unbelief is helping to build the bubble because it comes as a direct result of what you've been dwelling on. But the "demonic" or "evil" part is really a non-starter because the shadowy things begin with a thought. And whose head is that thought in? Yours! And because you are powerfully and wonderfully made in the image of an unstoppable love that isn't controlling your thoughts, you have the freedom to choose what you think about. Isn't that wonderful?"

"Ok? Wonderful? I don't know how wonderful it is when my thoughts seem to wander all over the place sometimes. Yes, I see what you're saying more clearly now, but is it really as simple as keeping my thoughts on things that are good and true? Are you saying that my thoughts are keeping me from receiving good things more than some evil force is trying to keep them from coming into my life?" I quipped.

"Yes, that's what I am saying to you. You are what you think. If you dwell on all that is difficult, hard, painful, boring, resentful, frustrating, and bad, then unconsciously your body will begin to follow through with those thoughts until resistance to what is good takes hold. On the contrary, if you think upon things that are good, true, fun, creative, lovely, and of value, then your heart will be at peace and the shield of resistance will come down. This is when it gets really fun! The good stuff will begin to have access to your life. The wall of separation will give way to the wide-open possibilities and blessings I have for you. They will chase you down and begin to overtake you at any moment of any day. This is where I get really happy because I get to surprise you, and I love surprises! I love bouncy houses too, don't you? They are so much fun when you joyfully trust like a child" Jesus said with a smile.

My mind was floored once more knowing this kind of mentality was true in my own life. Now I was starting to understand more of the depth of what it means to have the mind of Christ. If he doesn't dwell on negative things, then why should I? I was thinking about what that must look like being one with him on a moment-by-moment basis. I started to chuckle and throw up in my mouth a little at the same time at the thought of it.

Jesus responded, "Ah, no worries my friend! It's not like I will ever leave or forsake you! You are mine and I am yours for eternity! We have eternity to shift things! I'm enjoying helping you to see just how powerful you are and how brilliant your mind is! Keep bouncing with me! It will help to shake some of that plaque loose from the inside of your head so that you can think more clearly. Your "Spiritual lymphatic system" is bouncing to bring healing to your soul. I can see it happening even now and you are gonna love the results. In fact, that tinnitus you've been struggling with is disappearing the more you allow the bounce of trust to permeate your thoughts."

"Wow! He's right! I've been so clogged up with concerns and comfort foods that I couldn't think clear enough to feel the fullness of his love internally for me when I was in need. How could I allow my thoughts to bind me to the point of resisting his goodness? I mean, I thought I was doing the "right" thing by asking and trying to do his will! Why haven't I experienced the prosperous life I've always desired? I've been looking at trust like a burden because it turned into effort. I felt like if I crossed all my "T's" and dotted all my "I's" just right then he would give me all the good things in life! Man! What a hard way to live! I've been so exhausted most of the time trying to appease a God who just doesn't want or need it.

I am however, feeling more relieved with every bounce! Thank you Jesus! I can see clearly now that effort is gone! I sang with relief.

"Hey, that's it! You're getting it! That's a catchy song too! I can see clearly now that effort is gone. It's gonna be a bright, bright, sunshiny life!" Jesus sang in perfect tune and then started laughing like a child getting tickled.

His laugh was so contagious I started to bust out laughing too. So much so, I fell straight into the wall of my own pulsating artery. The more I laughed with him the more I felt my heart relax and melt right into his. I could hear the pounding of my heart begin to subside with relief. The bouncing turned into laughter, then to rest, and the rest turned into joyful tears of adoration for such a beautiful exchange. What a moment, what a God, what a safe friend we have in him.

When Jesus caught his breath from laughing so hard, he waved me forward to go further into the artery. He said, "Once you reach the interior of trust, that is when you know you're home. It's no longer a guess or a wish. It's an absolute knowing. The center of trust is the center of the heart and the heart is where you came from my friend. It's the very place where life resides, and the place where fear and death cannot co-exist. Come, follow me in, I have much more to show you."

I had a strong feeling that I would see many more mind-blowing things that would answer the fears I had before breathing through the "blood" of the artery. Not to mention all of the fears I've had over the years questioning my own heavy breathing through self-efforted attempts at doing life. With God it's always about more than meets the physical eye. It's about growth and maturing as we walk and talk together on a moment-by-moment basis. This encounter is certainly one of those life changing moments that is transforming how I believe. It's hard to imagine just how long I've been draining my own strength trying to make something happen. Following Jesus into the depth of trust keeps me thinking how effortless this all feels to my mind and soul. Yet my body seems uncomfortable with it, because I've been so used to striving to take care of my own needs and then calling it God.

As I followed him down the "bouncy house" corridor of trust, I couldn't help but think how much fun it was to bounce and laugh with him. It really does remind me of a child laughing when they get to experience a literal bouncy house in their backyard on their birthday. They don't have a care in the world while they're jumping away having fun receiving the joy of play.

Hearing my thoughts, Jesus stopped, turned, and said, "Oh yes,

now you're onto to something very powerful. The feeling you felt a few seconds ago was like taking on the trust of a child's emotion without really even thinking about it. This is what I meant when I said, "Unless you become like a child you will not be able to enter, comprehend, or see how the Kingdom operates. The very pillars of this realm and the heart you've entered into are founded on innocence, vulnerability, love, joy, and peace. That is all a child knows how to be. The joy they receive from having fun with their friends in the bouncy house is all that matters to them in the moment. It's all for the joy of it. If adults would simply play more throughout their day, then every day would be a birthday celebration of non-resistant fun.

Creativity Is Who You Are

"When a person has a mindset of play, then they remain in receiving mode. When you remain in a receiving mentality by simply feeling joy, that's when things become really adventurous and fun. You

literally become a moving frequency of creativity,
because creativity is the byproduct of joy."

Jesus continued, "A person cannot help but to exude creativity because it's who they are internally. Think of how creative a child is when they begin to rummage through a box of toys. Their imagination runs wild with possibility. They get lost in the moment of play creating worlds of fun. And this is when provision comes knocking on their door. Mom, dad, grandma, grandpa, or some other guardian comes into their room and says, "Ok sweetie, it's time for dinner!"

The provision of food comes and chases them down without them ever having to ask for it. Most of the time you have to literally pry a child away from their toys to feed them. This is why I said, "I have food you know not of". You see, food and every other need is not something to be idolized or even sought after with effort. Having your needs met is actually a result of getting lost in creative play. When play is engaged it sends a nonresistant signal out to the atmosphere to call for its match to manifest. That is when goodness shows up effortlessly in many different ways.

Do you remember how you felt a few minutes ago? Your laughter actually superseded your need to feel unworthy or unacceptable of receiving wonderful things. All you were doing is yielding to the laughter and joy of bouncing with someone else who was doing the same. It is my desire to see everyone live like this throughout their day. But some people may say, "Yes, that's nice for you Jesus, but I am human, and I have issues! I also have to work a job for ten hours and then come home to do it all over again with the kids!"

And I would respond by asking a few questions, "What issues? Does a child walk around all day feeling unworthy? Do they feel they have so many issues that it keeps them from their fun? Or do they simply run and dive into the bouncy house to play without any effort involved? Can you take on an attitude of play within your mind and soul while you are at your job? Even if you have a serious job that is filled with risk, can you shift your will to be lighthearted with your coworkers enough to keep them from harming themselves by being too rigid?

In other words, what I am saying is the power of non-resistance within someone is more powerful than you know. It can also be mentally engaged at any moment of any day. Playfulness is literally a spiritual magnet that attracts provision in a myriad of ways, but all it takes is the simple the will to turn it on to receive.

> *"When a child sees a colorful, bouncy house sitting in a yard, they automatically know that play is their natural state of being. Likewise, when an adult yields to their alignment in life, they too discover that fun and adventure are their inheritance now and forever."*

You see, sometimes we create our own strings of self-sabotage and unworthiness by believing we have to create some kind of formula in order to receive something good. Or we feel shame to the point of disappointment believing we can't trust that a "bouncy house" was given to us all because of love.

Let me ask you, my friend, did you have to do anything for me to take you on this adventure?" Jesus said with a sassy smile. "Umm no, I don't think so. But what about all those scripture verses that say I need to give in order to get, sowing and reaping, and the one in the book of Luke where it says, "Give and it shall be given?", and?"

Before I could say any more, the look on His face and the tears filling his eyes said it all. I noticed Jesus welling up with tears while I was giving all of my excuses. "Oh, man! Did I say something wrong?" I asked with a sinking feeling.

Jesus answered, "Wrong? No, nothing you are saying is wrong, but the word "wrong" is. You see, this is part of the larger issue with the Tree of Knowledge mentality. It lives intertwined with a right versus wrong mindset when it comes to relationship with me. When a person believes there's a right way and a wrong way to do something, then it causes them to live in fear and fear doesn't dwell in the Tree of Life where joy is ever-present. Play is the substance of things joyed for. In other words, when you live, move, and have your thoughts focused on joy, then the give-to-get formula is nowhere to be found. Many people believe that it's necessary to give something first in order to receive something they want or need from me. But since when did you ever stand around trying to give a gift to someone on your birthday just hoping the formula would work to get another gift in return? That's pretty silly, isn't it?

"But, but, but.." I was trying to justify all those sermons and scriptures in my head about how we are supposedly supposed to get things.

"But what?" Jesus said and turned to walk down the artery.
"But I thought you only provided for those who had faith in you and gave tithe money or helped the poor in some way?" I said sheepishly with my trained evangelical tone. (*I caught myself and it actually sounded a little creepy, like a fake, radio-disc-jockey trying to promote a product.*)

Jesus responded, "That's what many believe, don't they? Let me just say this; If I only provided for those who had enough faith, then why did I provide a bounty of wonderfully tasty bread and fish for all who hadn't even heard what I had to say yet? I fed thousands and healed many more before they ever became aware that my heart was in fact, pumping theirs? I was simply revealing my goodness to humanity because it's who I am. It never once crossed my mind that I required a love offering or a monetary exchange for giving 9,900 people some lunch.

Notice how I gave every single person a heartbeat before they even had the awareness to give anything? My love carried them in their mother's womb unobstructed by self-effort of any kind. Every child feels my adoration each and every moment of their formation. They begin to lose that knowing when their little minds become clouded as they grow up in environments of constriction.

My desire is that creation would live the life of playful surrender the rest of their existence, abiding in the Tree of Life intertwined with me. The reason you don't live this way is because ego is magnified under the tree of knowledge conditioning, blinding the mind from seeing that I am the source of love and all that is good.

"Humanity would rather work for something they believe they need, instead of receiving effortless provision through the love that empowers them to playfully create."

Love never requires you to earn what has always been freely given, and that includes money. It's just difficult for some people to believe I would provide without condition. Again, that is the obstruction and constriction of what ego provides through fear and panic."

"Omg! Wow! I've always somehow known you were this good, but the survivalist and religious conditioning in me has kept me running in circles, believing I had to work hard for everything!"

I shouted as unbelief continued to fall away.

"Omg" Does that stand for "Opulence. Mentality. Growing?" Jesus laughed as he lovingly played with my lingo.

"Yes, that's what it means!" I said smiling, knowing that he knew I was in fact, starting to comprehend what he was showing me. It never ceases to amaze me how kind and witty he is. It's not like he's ever clueless when it comes to human lingo. So many people think he is this huge stoic, stuffy, figure in the sky who lacks a sense of humor. Man, will they be surprised when they cross over into the reality of their heavenly existence! Not only am I experiencing the lighthearted, fun-loving nature of Jesus in this moment, I can tell you that he is the very one who gave us a sense of humor, to begin with. I am so grateful that I can converse with him the same way I would with my best friend in the natural. He's not put off by my personality in the least. In fact, he longs for his friends to be just that, authentic friends.

"Let's continue on" Jesus whispered. "I want to show you what trust looks like when you move toward the epicenter of all life."

Immersion Keeps Doubt From Taking Root

By now I had all but forgotten about the need for "normal" air in my lungs. It was now second nature to breathe in the words

and presence of his very life. I now have a little more under-standing of what it means to spiritually breathe "underwater". I mean, if a baby can literally do it in their momma's womb, then there's something powerful to be said about breathing Heaven's oxygen on earth. Everything Jesus is saying and doing in this moment reminds me of the first time I put on scuba gear, stuck an air regulator in my mouth, and sunk below the surface of the water to breathe for a while. At first, it felt a little intimidating and foreign to my body, but it didn't take long to feel like home. Everything under the surface of the water became surreal, peaceful, joyful, safe, and calming. Hearing your breath and heartbeat makes you feel very present. I can see why he said it's like being in your mother's womb; it's home because home is where momma's safe heart is.

On the flip side, some people just can't get used to breathing underwater when they try to scuba dive. That's because fear has overtaken their ability to breathe from another source. The mind tells the body to remain separated from the oxygen that is freely provided in the moment. It's what I like to call "oxygen dualism". Dualism is the in-between space that invites fear in to tell ego to protect itself, because it feels alone. But that never works inside the womb. There is no such thing as "dualism" inside a mother's womb. Oh yes, they are in fact separate beings, but they are joined as one through the umbilical cord.

The fifteenth chapter of the book of John in the Bible is a great pictorial of what union looks like with the Vine and branches illustration...

"I am the sprouting vine and you're my branches. As you live in union with me as your source, fruitfulness will stream from within you—but when you live separated from me you are powerless."

Jesus responded to my thoughts saying, "The only way to overcome this "separation" mentality is through immersion. Immersion into trust. The kind that can always be trusted to supply every ounce of oxygen needed to thrive in times of uncertainty. It's not a formula nor is it something you have to think long and hard about. It is simply the outcome of knowing how much you are adored.

Think about it my friend, a baby only "knows" one thing...love. But the baby doesn't necessarily have knowledge yet, because pure innocence doesn't require knowledge. Pure innocence is pure consciousness and pure consciousness is the absence of living from a right versus wrong mentality. The "reward versus punishment" kind of knowledge found in the diet produced by the Tree of Knowledge. Children eat the nourishment of fun, and they absorb the knowledge we give them. They don't have a concept of what it means to live a transactionary life like grown-ups do. They lose the innocence of receiving when they begin to absorb a skewed knowledge of survival through a parental figure.

Love is trusting that everything is already handled. The only "job" of a child is to rest, have fun, and grow in that love. When they begin to absorb the knowledge of an adult, that is when they become conditioned to think a certain way." Jesus said with resolve.

Wow! Now, isn't that interesting that God would give humanity the process of childbearing as an example of how he provides everything needed in life? It's simply a matter of becoming aware of the now and surrendering to the place of innocent trust again. The way in is playful, childlike faith. It's no wonder Jesus said things like, *"Don't stop the little children from coming to me, for such is the kingdom of God."* He was talking about innocent trust that is continuously yielding through presence, rest, and play. Think of the joy a mother has when she feels her baby kick for the first time in her womb. It's no wonder she says things like, "Oh look! He's playing!" every time the baby moves. Could this possibly be a clue as to what God has been trying to say to humanity all along? Hmm, it makes you truly wonder.

I can tell you this, every time I've gotten stressed out about money or provision, I've felt the Lord prompt me to go out and "play" so that I can forget about the problem for a while. Whenever I do, it seems the answer mysteriously appears in some form or another. It's amazing how that works, isn't it? Letting go of resistance to the default of the non-resistant nature of how life began, is far more powerful than human effort and striving could ever be. It's because Love himself loves to provide for us free of strings and manipulation. Isn't that what any good father or friend would do? Of course, they would!

My mind was racing with these truths, causing joy to over whelm me with the thought of living life in complete freedom. As I pondered some more, an opening appeared in the artery giving way to the most magnificent, beautiful, wondrous, glorious scene one could ever lay eyes on. It was like we were now entering a whole new world that looked like Jurassic Park (without the scary stuff) on steroids.

"What is this place?" I exclaimed with amazement.

"You have just entered the twilight zone!" Jesus jokingly said in a deep tone.

"Haha very funny!" I said with laughter. "No, seriously, what is this magnificent place?"

"It is the center of the human heart" Jesus said.

"Wuuut? No way! The human heart? This is not what I imagined it to be! I was told by religion that it was desperately wicked! This is far from evil! It's beautiful! Why would the Bible even say that the heart is desperately wicked? I don't understand!" I spouted with a troubling tone.

Jesus responded, "Ah yes, that one. That's the verse that has taken many people down the road of the reward versus punishment theology. Let me ask you, if the heart is evil, then why are you being led by it? The "Wicked" part the scripture is referring to is speaking of the spiritual condition man places themselves in through their own egoic thoughts and actions. It's illusionary. It has nothing to do with the beauty of what the heart actually is. The spiritual heart we are speaking of is the very atmosphere of presence, where safety is found. The heart isn't "desperately wicked". It's a matter of perception and then making a decision based upon that perception. This is where deception begins to take hold. If a person believes their own heart is evil, then shame opens the door to choose a path.

◆ ◆ ◆

Eden; The Place Where We Are Fully Known

Do you remember when we were talking about the shadow on the ceiling earlier? That was the shadow of decision. It wasn't my choice to see Adam do what he did, it was his. The beauty you are seeing here in front of you is Eden. This is the atmosphere of my presence and the place we call home. It's our dwelling place in man; the center of the heart."

"It is?? This is Eden? Wait a minute! I thought Eden was a physical place on earth where Adam and Eve lived thousands of years ago! How can Eden be in the center of the heart?" I said with a bewildered look.

Jesus responded, "Eden is the spiritual realm of tangible love. It's the place where everything living resides. It's a part of Heaven on earth abiding in the earth suit of man. This is the place where everything good resides and the place where you can really be you without fear of anyone else's opinion or judgments. Holy vulnerability and authenticity are found here. Isn't it gorgeous?

It's all authentically you and it's our home together!"

"Wow! Are you telling me this is really what everyone's heart looks like? This is breathtaking! There are no words!" I sparked with joy.

The entrance to Eden was glowing with a beautiful, dense, glitter-like substance. It looked to be made out of millions of crushed diamonds, rubies, emeralds, pearls, and every other kind of gemstone.

"Swoosh!"

A dust-like substance exploded and swirled around us. It looked as if it came straight out of the interior of the "walls" and "floor" of the opening. The "dust" surrounding us kept bouncing up in the air as if it was dancing. It was thick and "alive" as if millions of particles were desiring to be absorbed into your skin every time you breathed in. It didn't feel strange at all because I could sense they were filled with joy. They were obviously attached to the heart for a reason. It was so fascinating to me. In a small way, it reminded me of the glowing flowers and plant life in the movie Avatar, only a million times more beautiful and filled with a plethora of color I had never seen before.

"What is this beautiful, shimmering substance?" I asked.

"That my friend is what tangible trust looks like when you've entered into the abiding rest of trust. When a person lets the worry-filled walls of their own survival lifestyle down, this is what happens. You begin to enter the dance of the eternal realm of beautiful safety and care. In other words, you have now engaged the realm of well-being as you allow me to lead you in the dance. Every time you breathe in trust at the child-like level, the particles of trust begin to form and dance around you with a desire to bring security to that part of your life thatfeels unsafe and unstable.

People love shiny things. There is a reason people love to dress up in glittery clothes when they go to a ballroom dance, right? Where do you think they got that idea from? It all came from here, the substance of the heart of the matter. You see, dance is the one thing people do that reminds them of the spiritual realm they came from. Some are conscious of it, while others are not. It's all about flow and rhythm is a direct result of letting go to receive the substance of trust. Once you've allowed the flow of trust to be your anchor, then provision is as near as your breath.

It's the very dance I created the cosmos with, and the one we've been engaging humanity with throughout eternity. I mean, after all, you are made of stardust, right?? Jesus chuckled.

"Whoa! That is deep!" I thought. I was speechless and felt like I was just beginning to learn about the heart, but I could totally relate with the dance part. Not only do I love to watch people dance, but I have also always enjoyed doing it. It makes so much sense to me that whenever someone feels good, they feel like dancing in some form or another. Just look at all those people dancing to music in their cars as they cruise down the highway. It's not even about how good we think we can dance; the point is it comes straight out of Heaven and flows through our hearts whenever we feel a sense of happiness, joy, or excitement.

The Joy Of Rhythm

I kept pondering the significance of what this meant to Jesus and humanity as a whole. Wow! If everyone knew that God actually smiles upon dance, then perhaps the world would loosen up a little to come and join the party, even in the midst of adversity or some kind of pandemic.

"Yes! I love that!" Jesus rejoiced with a shout while doing a little dance jig. "You know why people don't dance more?" Jesus asked as he spun around in a circle.

"No, why?" I asked.

"Because their mind has become paralyzed with intellectual reasoning through conditioning, which causes them to stay off the dance floor of life. You see, when people feel good, they have transitioned from their lofty, tormenting thoughts to the non-resistant "free fall" eighteen inches down to the heart-centered dance floor of play. The interesting part is many people don't even realize they've made the transition when they do this. What they have done is moved from resistant thought to non-resistant feeling.

Ever notice when you think too much you don't have much rhythm or flow? You're stuck in an intellectual straight jacket. Try wearing one of those on a natural dance floor and feel how your rhythm is affected. In fact, people would say something like, "That boy doesn't know how to dance. He doesn't have any rhythm. Look how bound up he is! He crazy! Somebody needs to go help that boy!" Jesus laughed with humility.

"Yes, that was certainly "straight" to the point!" I said sarcastically.

Jesus continued, "Think about it this way. Whether people believe it or not they all have rhythm. It's in their veins, it's in their anatomy and it's in their thought life. Remember when I said that it was all "downstream" from here? That's because the path of trust is all "downhill" flowing straight into the rhythm of Eden, the place where everything is taken care of.

In fact, downstream is the flow that leads to an enormous ocean of abundance. Picture in your mind a spring flowing out of a mountain. That spring begins with pure, fresh, sparkling water, but then as it makes its way through the hills and into populated areas, it encounters waste left by humanity.

It's the same way with the mind. When thoughts begin to go downstream *(because everything always does naturally)* and then a person engages intellectual resistance to what is naturally flowing, things begin to cloud and clog. Dams begin to build, and resistance starts to pollute freshwater, much like a stagnant pond because it's blocked with resistance. But what's even more resistant is anchoring negative thoughts through reasoning. It's like having a backedup lymphatic system. Eventually, something has to give in order for the "sewage" build up to begin to flow down and out of the body. Non-resistant, happy thoughts keep everything flowing smoothly.

Another way to see it is to look no further than the human heart. If you were to go against the natural flow within the arteries of the heart, what would happen? That would be called blockage, and I think you know what comes next. In the same way, there is a rhythm and flow to everything in creation, as well as the spirit realm. When you try to go against the flow of what is, that's when things begin to work against you instead of for you." Jesus said as he moved his hand in the air like a break/pop dancer would to start a "Pop" move.

Laughing, I responded, "Ok, that makes sense. Are saying to just go with the flow then?"

"Yes, that is what I am saying. It doesn't mean that you just let anything, and everything happen within you or to you because your thoughts are the stream that begins the flow. And they will eventually become an ocean of abundance in your life, good or bad.

Trust is not inactivity. Remember, faith is substance and the evidence of things that come to you. They work for or against you, depending on where your thoughts are pooling or flowing. "Going with the flow" as you say, is allowing the natural pull of my love to take you downstream to where trust turns into Eden. And Eden is an ocean of abundance without any strings attached. Except those of the heart that aren't really strings, but more like arteries…lol. When you sync into Eden through thought and emotion, they pull on my heartstrings making us want to dance with you even more! We love to dance with you. We like to call it the "Downstream Dance" … Jesus said as he tapped his toe back and forth on the floor of the artery.

◆ ◆ ◆

The Dam Of Stress

While Jesus was sharing, I don't know why, but I had this funny picture in my mind of a one-toothed beaver sitting there just staring at me. It was puzzling at first, but then I quickly realized that sometimes my thoughts cause me to look like that beaver missing a tooth because he was chewing so hard on his thoughts. It was really a mirror reflection of my own striving. I had been so dammed up at times with stress that I didn't even realize that downstream was where I was supposed to be headed. I was taught that I need to work hard fighting upstream for everything I wanted and needed because downstream was being lazy or simply giving up. Man, what a way to live, eh? I thought to myself as I continued to laugh at the toothless beaver inside my head.

"Yep, it's funny to think about it now, right?" Jesus quipped with a clear understanding of what upstream thinking is like. "Perhaps it's time to walk away from the Leave it to Beaver Show, eh?" He said with a humorous tone.

"Haha! Yes! Yes, it is time." I said with laughter.

"Ok, are you ready to see more of your new, yet not so new

home?" Jesus said with excitement.

"Yes! I am so ready!" I said with relief. I was ready to move past

the picture of a one tooth wonder of a beaver and that dam imagery in my head.

As we walked across to the other side of the entrance to Eden suddenly we were standing high up on a mountain top looking "down" at the center of the heart. It seemed like it was thousands of feet deep with no ending. It was that big. It was spectacular in every way, and difficult to put into words the magnificence I was beholding. I stood there in awe at the sight and wanted to take it all in forever.

"Follow me and get ready for the ride of your life!" Jesus said while rubbing his hands together.

The Slide That Changes Perspectives

No sooner than he said that, a huge slide appeared in front of us; a great big red one, that any child would drool over.

"A slide? Wow! I love slides!" I thought as excitement flooded my soul. It was like I was seven years old again. I couldn't believe there was an actual slide inside the heart.

What could this mean? I pondered as I followed Jesus over to the top of the slide. He was giddy with excitement as well. You could tell this meant a lot to him by the way he was dancing and jumping around like a small child getting ready to have the greatest time of his life. His joy was contagious. I couldn't help but dance and shout alongside of him as we looked down over the edge. It was kind of intimidating, but I had complete trust knowing he was and is the very source of fun and safety.

"Ok, let's hold up for a minute or so. Before we slide into the depths of Eden, let's take another look at this beautiful view of Mt. Heaven." Jesus said as sweat rolled off his forehead from all the excitement.

"Wait! What? We're standing on a "mountain" called Heaven? Can't be! I thought you said this was Eden and the heart of humanity? Heaven is a mountain too? How could it be?" I said with confusion in my tone.

"Yes, to all three! What you are looking at is the wide-open expanse of my never-ending presence. It's everywhere and permeates all things. There is nowhere that it's not and nowhere that I am not. Heaven is not a literal mountain you gaze upon or climb. Heaven is the very internal substance you are made of and the one you breathe in. Mt. Heaven is another name for the tangibility of my presence, while Eden is the atmosphere that surrounds it. In other words, you are surrounded in oneness with all that I am. You can't escape it. My presence is the very desire of the nations. Some people just don't know that yet, but they will. When they get tired of climbing their own mountains of effort, they'll let go and slide into the effortless flow of my heart intertwined with theirs." Jesus said with assurance.

"This is all too wonderful to me! So, if Mt. Heaven is your presence and Eden is the atmosphere, then are they both considered the same thing? They're both filled with such beauty and I can't tell the difference! If they are the same, then why have I been taught they are different?" I asked. (My curiosity couldn't help but want to know the answer).

"Yes, they are one in the same, because it's all love. I have always made it a point to give man signposts along their journey to help them see and experience my presence wherever they are. For it's the high places that man desires and I have always met humanity in their own pursuits to either seek after me or strive to have influence of their own. When people reach the summit of their own egoic desire, they will either find rest knowing it was I who drew them there to reveal something to them, or they will become frustrated and confused in their own self-efforts. Either way, Mt. Heaven and Eden are both there waiting internally to show them where the slide is when they get tired of climbing up something that was never meant to be done in their own strength.

In other words, life was never meant to be an uphill struggle. It has always been a downstream reality in the effortless world of Spirit. When people get tired of holding on to their climbing rope of their own security, the only alternative is to let go and

flow where the gravity of my Spirit is taking them.

> *"Life is so much easier and a lot more fun when flow is happening, especially when the rush of spiritual adrenaline creates an expectancy that things will always work together for your good."*

Jesus continued...

That's why the heart itself is filled with ease. Have you ever noticed in the natural that when you genuinely let go of a fear or an anxiety, you begin to experience an immediate relief to your physical heart? The rhythm of calm comes back to relieve the upward climb. And why is that? It's because letting go to sync or "slide" into playful trust causes you to engage Eden once again.

Now, just so we are clear, we are not talking about going back to an "after the fall" type of Eden scenario where Adam struggled. I am talking about the Eden that has always been present. It's the Eden of my presence that has no beginning and no ending. Tell me, does the place you are standing in right now feel like the now? Or does it look and feel like you are taking in a mere Bible history lesson on a particular subject?" Jesus asked with a somewhat sarcastic tone.

"It certainly feels current or present. This is definitely not old, I mean, ancient feeling. Is that the right word?" I didn't know how to articulate it in the moment.

"That's ok, I know what you mean. The truth is my friend, it's eternal, and its current because Eden and Mt. Heaven live in and around you now. You are not only one with them, but they are the realm of love...the very life flow you are created with. Remember, *home is where the heart is, and heart is where home is*. When humanity gets completely weary of living the illusion of life on their own terms, they will come running back home. Once they let go of their own efforts then the warmth of the sand begins to call them towards their own journey back towards the center of the heart. Once that happens, they will be drawn down the artery to experience the substance of the "dust of trust" to join you and I for the ride of a lifetime.

Letting go to sync into playful trust even for a moment, reminds a person of their spiritual home, the place they originate from. Trying to figure it out on your own is like climbing a mountain that was meant to be slid down. That's what downhill looks like and that's what Eden feels like. Are you ready?

Let's go for a slide!" Jesus shouted.

All I could do was fall more in love with this God who knew every part of me as I prepared to follow his lead.

"Yes! I'm ready! Let's go!" I exclaimed as I closely followed him down the slide. "Wahoooo! This is awesome!" I shouted as we twisted and turned down the slide together. I was having so much fun feeling like a child again. Jesus was having a blast too. I watched from behind as he threw his hands in the air like someone riding on a roller coaster. He even shouted, "Throw your hands in the air like you just don't care!" as he rounded a turn.

I lost it. I was crying so hard I could barely breathe, but at the same time, I was having bouts of laughter too. It was truly amazing, and I didn't want it to end. It was so healing for my soul in every way. This is the Jesus I always knew to be true. This was the friend that sticks closer than a brother. He is the very definition of fun and adventure. How did I allow my mind to take me so far away from who I've always known him to be deep down?

It's like time stopped as I twisted and turned my way down the slide behind Jesus. I couldn't help but think about how his love changed my life many years ago, yet it's still dramatically changing it now.

Life is interesting, isn't it? When we first become aware of his presence through some kind of encounter in life, his love is all we can think about. It's all we long for and it's all we need. But then life happens, our minds remind us of the past, bills appear, jobs take over, religion creeps in and the grind starts to overwhelm us. And then we ask ourselves, "How did we ever get here?".

Following Jesus down the slide of bliss was like being inside a slow-motion movie. It's making me realize what is really important in life. Seeing his hands in the air having fun like a child changed everything for me. I was utterly lost in time and didn't have a care in the world. I could tell he was enjoying every second of his time with me too. All I wanted was to take in the sheer pleasure of watching Jesus laugh his way down the slide.

Isn't that what life is supposed to be like? I don't know about you, but I need a lot more fun in my life, and this experience has awakened the child in me that I never wanted to force to grow up, to begin with. I have found that when we have a mentality that causes us to believe that Jesus doesn't laugh hysterically or would ever want to have fun going down a slide, then perhaps it's time to change our belief about who he really is. It's not like I manufactured this encounter with him in order to feel better about myself. No, it's all real and our spirit man knows when something is true. When a person experiences the smile and laughter of God, it's a real game-changer.

As we laughed our way down the slide, I noticed we kept gaining speed. We went from slow motion to fast forward in a few seconds. It felt like we were moving into some kind of accelerated hyperdrive. I could feel my skin pulling back like it would with someone sitting in a flight simulator training to become a jet pilot. We were flying so fast I felt like we were going to break through to the other side of another galaxy somewhere. As soon as I rounded another turn I heard a thunderous splash in front of me.

◆ ◆ ◆

Immersed In Spirit

"Splash!"

I saw Jesus hit what looked to be like water.

"Splash!"

There I went right behind him.

I immediately felt warmth all around me likened to warm, tropical water you would find in Hawaii or some other paradise. It felt wonderful. The "water" surrounded me as I came up for "air". But I found out very quickly I didn't need regular air like I thought I needed a while ago while entering the artery. It kind of shocked me as to why I didn't need it and why we hit the water with such velocity. It's not like it hurt or anything. I wasn't in pain like you normally would be jumping off some 30-foot cliff into a lake landing on your stomach. No, this was like hitting a "pillowy soft" substance.

It felt so good that I went under the surface again just to take in another breath. I was so confounded that I could breathe "underwater". As soon as I went back under and opened my eyes, I could hardly believe what I was seeing. On the "bottom" of this "ocean" or whatever this was, there were what looked to be like millions of gemstones beaming with shimmering light in every direction. They were blindingly radiant and seemed to be moving. Upon seeing them I immediately shot back to the surface and shouted, "Wow! Amazing! It's so beautiful down

there! This is so wonderful! What is this place?"

Jesus laughed while treading "water" and said, "This is the Crystal Sea of Spirit in the heart of Eden. What we slid into was the substance of pure Spirit. What you feel is the warmth of my Spirit enveloping yours. Isn't it awesome?"

"Yes! Yes! Yes! I love this! I could stay here forever! I've never felt more at home! This fits me! Wow!" I shouted with fervor.

I couldn't help but be overcome by emotion. I laughed and cried some more. Great tears of overwhelming joy flooded my soul as I splashed through the wonderful "water" of Spirit.

"So, is this the Spirit of who I am too? It feels so much like me! Like what I know myself to be without any limitations. I feel… feel, like I'm invincible!" I shouted with overwhelming joy.

Jesus responded, "Yes, it is very much who you are as well.

There is no separation between you and I, my friend. I am in you and you are in me and love surrounds us throughout eternity. Have you noticed we are both swimming around in the wonder of this endless pool of Spirit and my head is level with yours?"

"Yes! I see that." I said with joy.

"That's because there's only one mind in this place. The mind of Spirit. There's no hierarchy in Spirit and there's no separation here. It's joint union. The water of the Spirit we are swimming in has no point of separation. It's all one. Isn't it amazing?" Jesus shouted.

"Yes! Wow! I can see it and feel it! It's so comforting here, and it feels so wonderful!" I exclaimed.

"Great! I'm glad you feel that way, because it's the place you came from and it's the very substance you dwell in. It's the womb of all life. It's your real home. And did you notice that just below your feet lay the opulence of what provision is like once you let it all sync in? All that is needed is complete surrender to "splash" into the fullness of Spirit. You've already discovered you can breathe under the surface. It's a reminder of what life was like in the womb. Go ahead! Dropdown into the depths of your own spirit and take a closer look at the gemstones of provision awaiting you!" Jesus exclaimed.

"Ha! Ha! I love this!!!!" I shouted from the top of my lungs. I kept saying it over and over again. "I love this! I love this! I love you Jesus!"

I was beside myself with adoration and gratitude for what I was experiencing. This felt so good that I could hardly stand or should I say, "swim" it. It felt like my entire being would explode into a million pieces of joy. I was excited and overwhelmed at the fact that I just slid down a supernatural slide of joy with Jesus and crashed into the Spirit of who I am in oneness with him.

The best part of all this? He was smiling and laughing the entire time. I can't tell you how transformative this is and was for me to experience with him. I had questioned whether or not he was in fact, smiling upon having so much fun watching me have fun discovering these truths about him. I mean, after all, this was the heart of humanity we were in! We were swimming around in the endless pool of Spirit having fun together! It is changing everything I ever knew about who he is to humanity. He loves deeply, and he passionately cares for all people. I was experiencing such elation at the thought that he wasn't focused on calling out some kind of "sin" in me. He was just loving on and having fun with me simply because I was with him.

◆ ◆ ◆

Breathing Underwater

"Ok, here I go! I'm going under!" I said with excitement.

I went under once more and let the breath out of my lungs to sink to the "bottom" of the sea. Or at least that's what I thought I was doing. *(It's difficult to describe how I could breathe underwater. Perhaps I let the air out due to habit in the natural.)* I was so excited for my feet to touch the beautiful gemstones. I kept sinking further and further down, but there was no "bottom" to be found. I didn't panic though because I could breathe. I just let the substance of Spirit take me further under. Fear was here to be found. It was nothing but safety, pure safety, all around me.

As I "fell" into the depth of Spirit, I looked "down" and noticed that some of the jewels were moving my way. They started to surround me. It was like they were alive and "swimming", kind of like you would see on a video where millions of fish swim together in a wave-like vortex in the ocean. It looked very much like that, only way more beautiful as their radiance flashed back and forth in the light of the "water". They were swimming in circles around me. All I could do was relax and enjoy this powerful moment. I didn't care what they were doing, nor did I frantically swim to the surface to ask Jesus what it all meant. I just took in their beauty because I knew Jesus wanted me to. He is the one who asked me to check them out to begin with. But as beautiful and mind-blowing as all of this opulence was, my heart just wanted to be near his to hear him laugh again.

As I pondered these things inside the vortex of the jewels, I began to feel significantly different inside. Something lifted off my mind. I heard a loud pop and then felt something drain down the inside of the back of my head. It was like something flushed from my mind and I could see more clearly than ever before. It wasn't a natural seeing, but a spiritual one. It's like I had brand new vision for the first time, and it felt really good.

I closed my eyes to feel more of this wonder surrounding me. I was suspended in the depth of the Spirit realm and felt right at home with an insight I had always longed for but didn't fully understand until now. I was beginning to see how provision is simply a matter of allowing ourselves to let go of resistance to the point of complete surrender in order to find our true selves immersed inside of ever-flowing provision. It was like I became an energetic match internally to the good that has always been surrounding me externally. This experience was extraordinary, yet familiar to me. I couldn't help but think I had died and gone to Heaven.

"Breathe it all in John!" I kept telling myself with deep satisfaction. I was immensely enjoying the feeling of what it was like to be fully immersed and one with Spirit.

As I continued to surrender to the moment, I heard the sound of thousands of jewels clashing together, followed by a loud swooshing sound in front of me. I opened my eyes and saw an opening in the vortex of gemstones. Jesus was there floating in the water. It was so surreal that I could see him so clearly. The "water" or Spirit realm was so clear in color it felt like we were standing on dry land.

Knowing my thoughts Jesus said, "That's because it's more real than dry land. The Spirit world is the real world. Everything else is an illusion in comparison."

I just "stood" there. I mean, "treaded" there for a moment staring at him. I was dumbfounded at how "normal" this all was. We were underneath the surface of another realm, yet the same world. It was as if it was all one.

Jesus laughingly responded, "It's all becoming "crystal clear" to you now, isn't it? The reason you haven't been able to see it until now is because of the resistance built up in your own understanding. Your belief has been like a dropped anchor attached to a boat. When the winds of Spirit start to move the vessel and the anchor is left dragging the bottom of the ocean. It stirs up the debris of unbelief clouding your perception from seeing where the Spirit wants to take you.

There is no resistance here. You are now allowing the Spirit to take you where it naturally flows. The eyes of your understanding are now beginning to open to a world that is familiar; the one we call home, your eternal home. It's also when natural things become "magnetic" and begin to swim towards you, because they too are void of resistance in this place."

"Wow! Ok, so is that why the jewels are surrounding me? It's like they are dancing or something! It's so beautiful!" I said with joy.

"Yes, that's exactly why they are dancing around you. Every thing dances in the Spirit realm because it's fully alive and able to move with effortlessness. They live in non-resistance to all that is good. The gemstones represent provision in every form imaginable. They are attracted to you because they are free to move towards that which matches their effortless nature.

People Who Don't Strive Are Safe

"The more someone offers themselves to creative content-ment, the more effortless provision will surround them, because the energy exuding from money is "excited" about giving itself to the safety of unforced creativity."

The gemstones are drawn like a magnet towards a person when they recognize a match. When you dropped underneath the surface at the sound of my voice you were completely at rest, offering no struggle to your surrender. It's not unlike the disciples when they felt my smile through my words and then dropped their nets into the non-resistant side of the boat. Abundance began to surround them because the fish recognized a match to the tangible frequency of effortlessness attached to the net. Created things that are flowing in their own authenticity immediately recognize other created things that are flowing in their own." Jesus said with confidence.

I was "floored" by his answer floating in the middle of my own suspension in the sea. Scripture verses kept rushing through my head about striving and the many scenarios in my own life where I worked so hard trying to make something happen.

"So, does this mean that hard work is the same thing as resistance? I see so many people working their brains out to make money. Is that how it's supposed to be? Scripture says that if we "don't work, we don't eat, right?" I asked with a not-so-sure tone. *(I wanted to hear directly from the Creator of all good things myself. I've been so wary of well-meaning people giving a myriad of inter-*

pretations of scripture verses relating to work and money over the years, so I was desperate to hear what Jesus had to say about it.)

"Ha! Ha! Ok, I know what you're meaning my friend. Are you ready? Here we go. Let's walk it back to the Garden of Eden story in the Bible. When I spoke planet earth into existence, it was the creation I had always imagined it to be. We saw it together and then spoke it out of the light that never stops creating. It's the same light as the Spirit you are floating in. When the light of my love brought forth the entire cosmos, everything was provided, including the provision needed for humanity on planet earth.

Now, for the sake of linear time here I won't go into detail, because I have much more to show you within the heart of humanity. But let's just say that what you are feeling and seeing here was the norm for Adam and Eve. Provision was already "magnetized" to them because prior to their decision to walk away from the ease of love and straight into effort, everything in their world was void of resistance.

In other words, imagine if I said this to Adam...

"Adam, I have given you a lot of responsibility and a whole lot of work to do. You're a smart guy, and I know you'll figure out how to create a shovel and plant clippers for all the work that is needed to tend to the Garden. I made you a gardener to care for all these plants, so take care of them to the best of your ability. It's going to be hard work, but I'll make sure to pay you with fruit from the trees after I hold a week's worth of pay out of your check. Your pay dates will be the 5th and 25th of each month. You won't have access to the fruit until then. If you need provision before the next paycheck, then you'll just have to fast because the payroll department doesn't issue checks until then.

Isn't that just the most ridiculous thing you've ever heard my friend?" Jesus said half chuckling.

"Umm, yes, totally! But it's not unlike many things I've experienced in the natural world of work. I guess people are just bent on abusing themselves into getting their needs met? It's all they know." I said with sarcasm mixed with sorrow.

"Yes, I do understand what you are saying, believe me. But Adam never had a job, title, position, or college degree to begin with. His only "job" if you want to call it that, was to stay in receive mode with life having fun enjoying creation and our time together. He didn't know anything else because he lived in the purity of innocence where provision is always present. The "gardener" part was merely tending to his own heart in relationship with me.

The broken veins on the wall inside the Artery of Trust were representative of a trust that was broken through resistance to that which is good. But when it comes to the purity of Eden, everything is connected flowing in harmonious peace because things are aligned with an optimal state of being. They are awakened with an ever-flowing peace that is saturated with effortless provision.

◆ ◆ ◆

Provision Was Already Present In The Garden

In the same way, provision was already flowing and present before Adam was given flesh and bone. Did you happen to notice in the story of Adam and Eve that he was transported in the Spirit by the Spirit to his dwelling place, while he was completely at rest? In other words, the magnetism of creation responded to his restful state and then drew him to the very atmosphere that was best "suited" for him. And that "place" was simply walking in union with me in the love of each and every day.

Everything Adam and Eve had need of or could ever want was given to them before they ever arrived in human form. Every bit of provision came packaged inside the light of Spirit and manifested into material form, because it was my good pleasure to give them the desires of their heart. Meaning, that when someone is in a state of rest matching the non-resistant nature of Spirit, there's an offering up of provision. It's the ground "Yielding its strength" to Adam. It's the nucleus of surrender "matching" non-resistance. It's the very substance you and I are conversing in and it's the very place I reached in to grab the gold bar from earlier. Once this understanding forms within you, then nothing is impossible. You can walk on water (*no pun intended*) and you can watch the miraculous unfold right in front of you.

Would you like to hear some more? Or are you good for now?" Jesus said with a smile.

"Yes! Wow! That is absolutely awesome! What's interesting is that I feel like I've known these truths deep inside of me all along. They sound so familiar to me. Yes! I want more, as much as you want to give me!" I said with bubbling epiphany.

"Is this why the jewels moved towards me? Was it because I was focused on you?" I asked.

"Yes, but it's also because you released your need for the want. Whenever you change your mind from the frequency of negativity over to appreciation and keep it there, that is when the magnetic pull starts to happen. Think about it this way. Why would anyone who is in a good mood want to purposely hang out with someone who is not, for any length of time? Remember the "Bad company corrupts good morals" scripture? It's a true statement.

It's the same thing with thoughts. Bad thoughts attract bad company. It's the ship tossed back and forth in the wind syndrome; where double-mindedness causes a pull to happen in both directions. They cancel each other out leaving nothing to happen. This is where people feel stuck, and numbness begins to set in. It's the place where stagnation takes hold and things start to stink. Isn't that why you say things like, "This stinks?" Jesus said while pinching his nose.

"Oh boy, you caught me. Yes, I have said that very same phrase many times throughout the years. That makes so much sense to me now about double-mindedness. That particular scripture verse in the book of James was somewhat confusing to me because it made it sound like you were the one withholding good things. I thought you were saying that I wouldn't receive anything from you if I remained double-minded! But my heart knows better! It was simply me living in contradiction to your mind." I said with emotion.

"Yes, my friend, you have known this all along because your spirit has known it all along. You're just now seeing it because your eyes have been opened to what you held to be true through someone else's interpretation. In fact, everyone knows life is effortless within their spirit. Someone just told them that it's too good to be true because they tried letting go once, and it didn't work for them. It's not that it didn't work, because it does and that's just it, there's no "work" involved here. How hard was it for you to follow me into the heart of humanity to see that Mt. Heaven isn't about "climbing" anything? It isn't about effort or striving. It's effortless. Love is effortless.

It's the same way with starting to observe all that is good and then losing the temptation to focus on something that is not. The more you practice the easier it becomes. You'll then begin to do what you see Love doing, which causes all good things to be attracted to you. Those things are waiting in the Spirit realm the moment you open your heart to receive them through joy. They show up in your physical world when you least expect them to. The only things a child "expects" in their little world is to have fun. They don't spend their time sitting around checking their email and bank accounts every hour. No, they simply engage the joy of the moment."

As Jesus finished his last sentence, every jewel surrounding me shimmered as if they were filled with laughter and play. It was the most amazing sound one could ever hear. Imagine millions of gemstones shimmering and "laughing" in unison as they listened to the sound of Love speak. It was as if they all had personalities or something. I could literally see the joy emanating from their beauty. This moment was truly mesmerizing. It was like I was in some kind of powerful dream and didn't want to wake up.

"Oh Jesus, keep me here forever with you!" I thought with such blissful contentment. Not because I was surrounded by such opulence alone, but because my mind and heart were being healed from skewed paradigms I had believed for so long. It didn't matter if the jewels remained or left my life forever. It was the conversation and demonstration about my own thinking that was priceless.

◆ ◆ ◆

Change Your Thoughts, Change Your Life

As I pondered the gravity of the moment, another question came to mind. "If changing our thoughts is so easy, then why don't people do it more?" I asked as Jesus played with the gemstones dancing around me.

"It's because they find it easier to think on things they are familiar with through their conditioning and life experiences. In general, people don't like change no matter how good it may seem. In the same way, it's like trying to convince someone to experience a different selection on a menu at a familiar restaurant. They would rather continue eating something their taste buds have become accustomed to because it brings them comfort in some way, and they don't want to be disappointed if another choice doesn't taste as good. This is what a survival mentality looks like. It looks appealing and tastes good while they are thinking about things of the past and future until they find out those thoughts are slowly killing them.

In other words, people who are only used to life a certain way, genuinely believe that is how life is supposed to be. Have you ever had a conversation with a friend about how you noticed they were being emotionally or physically abused by someone close to them, and they flat out denied it? It's frustrating to see, isn't it? It's because the taste of that kind of "food" has left them feeling somewhat satisfied enough to keep them from experiencing something else. This is what people call the "Survival mentality" or "Battered person" syndrome.

How many times have you heard your friends and acquaintances say things like, "Just give me enough money for a cup of coffee once and awhile and enough to pay my bills every month and I'm good. I don't need much to make me happy." While that may be somewhat of a "humble" statement and may in fact be true to them in the moment, it doesn't mean that it's the full truth. Yes, of course, they should be happy regardless of their circumstances, but what happens when they lose their job, and they can no longer buy that cup of coffee? Does it make them unhappy due to their perceived loss? Negative thoughts and emotion surrounding that cup of coffee then to turn into resistance, because they can't have their coffee when they want it. And why can't they buy it? Because their beliefs kept them in survival mode limiting them to a job and that cup of coffee.

In other words, was their happiness contingent on having a job and a cup of coffee every day? When that all goes away, where does that leave their thoughts? Right back to the limitations they have always known, eating the same kind of "food" they have always eaten and drinking the same cup of coffee they have always consumed. Thus, keeping beautiful magnetism far from their experience; even though the fullness of goodness was dancing right in front of them the whole time. Kind of like these jewels are doing now with you." Jesus said with compassion.

"That is great wisdom! So, does that mean that by shifting what we believe about what you think towards us, will cause us to be more non-resistant in our minds? Is this what you meant by having the mind of Christ?" I asked.

"Yes. Having the mind of Christ simply means that your emotions match your belief to all that is good and then remaining open to receive. You could say it's also the mind of the fruit of spirit…love, joy, peace, patience, goodness, kindness, faithfulness, longsuffering, and self-control. These are the elements of a spiritual recipe for putting you into a good mood and keeping you intertwined with receiving. When a person lives these things out in their mind every day, there is no law or "gravity" keeping them away from magnetism.

In other words, a mind flooded with the fruit of goodness keeps you open to receive more of the same. Provision is attracted to a mind that is filled with goodness. Love offers no resistance to all good things because it is good. The same goes for peace, joy, gentleness, and the rest.

The reason you are seeing these gemstones dance around you is because they feel "safe" enough to give themselves to someone who isn't trying to resist them through negative emotion and manipulation. Things like, "I don't deserve you" and "I never have any money" and "Why would God want to bless me with wealth" and "If I ever do get a lot of it I am going to chose who I think deserves it", and so on.

You were feeling good as you sunk underneath the surface into the depths of Spirit. You weren't analyzing your way under through intellectualism, fear, survival, negativity, and doubt.

Childlike trust in your own heart has led you to the doorway of Eden where anything is possible. Like I mentioned before, all children know how to do or want to do is play. In fact, the more a child joyfully plays the more joy fills the heart of a parent, causing them to want to provide even more fun for their child. Adventurous things as well, because there's an innate desire that is placed on the inside of every child and adult to want to discover new things.

Things like food, water, and treats are a mere byproduct of love. That is a given. But play, however, opens up the entire cosmos of imagination for the child and the adult to explore.

> *"Play is the doorway that opens the way for effortless provision to come in. Creative play paves the way to a brand-new day for all good things to come your way. So go play."*

You didn't see the dance coming, did you, my friend?" Jesus said with that familiar chuckle.

"No, you're right. I didn't see this coming. I am really lovingthis experience though! I don't ever want it to end." I said with wonder.

The jewels that were surrounding me now began to flow off into the distance. The sound of their movement was beautifully mesmerizing. You could feel the rush of their unity as they circled into a funnel and "swam" away. What an amazing moment and one I will never forget. Once they swirled away out of sight, Jesus was still floating there in front of me smiling. He was looking at me anticipating more questions. He loved answering them. I could tell by the way he smiled at me.

"Go ahead my friend, I'm here for you. Do you have another question?" He said with a grin.

"Yes, I do actually. I have many questions, but this one in particular still has me somewhat baffled. Obviously, I can't help but notice all of this extravagance and wealth surrounding me at every turn. From the massive diamond crashing into the sand, the gold bar coming out of thin air, the wad of cash you pulled out of the sky, the main entryway embedded with priceless gemstones, the gold veins in the wall, the jewel dust and millions of jewels dancing around me. It's all so overwhelming and all so unfamiliar in my own natural experience.

If this is so plentiful and easy to access, then why haven't I experienced more if it? Is it because I am not mature enough to handle it? I'm still not quite understanding it yet! Is it because I'm still living in the past? If it's just simply having a good attitude and thinking good thoughts, then shouldn't I at least be seeing a jewel drop out of thin air or a gold bar show up in my house once and a while?" I asked with a frustrated tone.

Jesus smiled and said, "Let me show you something that will help answer your questions. Come with me."

By now I knew enough to follow him, even though my mind couldn't quite comprehend the enormity of what he has already shown me. This is all very much like a wild dream that certainly takes you off guard, but one you do not want to wake up out of. It's what a person sees in their imagination when they daydream about what they would do if they won a billion-dollar lottery. Only this was far greater than some mere lottery. This was Jesus himself smiling, laughing, and approving of all this opulence found right here inside the spiritual heart of humanity.

There isn't enough money in the entire universe that could ever replace these conversations I'm having with him. After all, this was Jesus himself we are talking about. It would be much different if I were merely daydreaming about money and feeling guilty at the same time because of some hangup in my head about it. Jesus is simply revealing what Heaven is made of and what his presence is like in the midst of it all. It doesn't get any better than this. In other words, when Jesus shows you limitless wealth with a big smile on his face, it's a far different story than what man believes about it in their own skewed understanding. Religion and trauma have done a good job of keeping humanity in a place of want and lack be cause of survival mechanisms.

CHAMBER 2

Enter the Artery of Memory

A s we floated back "up" to the top of the Sea/Spirit I felt like a piece of me was left floating in the deep. It felt like I was leaving someone I loved and missing them already. My heart started to sink a little as we breached the surface together. It's not like my heart wasn't already full being with Jesus, it's just that there's a comfortable familiarity with immersion deep in Spirit.

"Splash!"

Suddenly, we broke the surface.

I looked over at Jesus and he was looking at me as if to say, "Wasn't that just crazy awesome?" Neither of us said a word for a few minutes. I knew he knew that what just happened in the deep was life-changing for me. It was like one of those moments where you stare at a best friend stunned with the wonder you just beheld together. Words cannot accurately describe what I just witnessed with my own spiritual eyes and heard with my own ears.

After breaking the surface of the "water" you would think you would need to draw in a big breath of air after having been down there so long, but it wasn't necessary. I was breathing underwater just as normal as I would be on the surface.

Answering my thoughts Jesus said, "Yes, it does feel like you are leaving a part of yourself down there. It feels that way because life in the Spirit is your home. You're not leaving this place at all;

you're just going to see another dimension of it. It's all one in the same yet separate in the way it all operates. Come with me and I'll show you more."

As we moved to the edge of the Crystal Sea, I followed Jesus out of the water to stand on the shore. I didn't have to walk out of the Spirit onto the shore, it was more like transitioning or translating out. Picture in your mind a particular scene in a movie fading into another one. When one scene moves to the next, they call it a transition. This is what it was like the entire time I was in the heart of humanity. It's like there were no barriers or limitations everywhere I followed him. No climbing, no sweating, and no heavy breathing from hard labor.

◆ ◆ ◆

Liquid Love

As I stood there pondering the depth of my interaction in the Spirit, I looked over and saw the big red slide off in the distance. It seemed like it was miles away, yet it was like I could reach out and touch it. I looked around some more taking in all the wonder of this place Jesus calls Eden and Mt. Heaven. Is there any ending to this magnificent place? I thought as we turned to walk towards what looked like a stairway going up from the shoreline. *(You may be wondering if we needed to dry off from being in the Spirit, but it wasn't like that at all. Yes, it did feel like liquid, but it wasn't. That's because the Spirit is liquid love. Spirit is there because you can hear "it" and feel it, but it doesn't leave any material matter or substance dripping off your body like water does. You simply breathe love in and breathe love out. Your spirit is the real substance of who you are. If you had x-ray eyes, for example, you would definitely be able to see it, but the more important thing is you can feel it. This is why emotions are so important. If we would simply learn to feel our way through life's experience overthinking our way, we would move in union with Spirit more frequently. We would begin to see, feel, and taste things that would transform our lives dramatically.)*

◆ ◆ ◆

Tv Memories

"Check this out!" Jesus blurted.

"Wow! Are those TV's?" I said as we walked up the stairs.

"Yes, they are TV screens. Take a look and tell me what you see." Jesus quipped. *(There were lots of Tv's lining each side of the stairs and they were all tuned to different channels. Some of the televisions looked like the old "boxy" kind we used to have before the credit card thin/narrow ones came out. Some were small and others were as big as movie screens, like the size you would see at a movie theater.)*

"Ok, I'm looking at them?" I said with reservation. Jesus was now about ten steps ahead of me.

"I recognize that show! That's Sesame Street! Ha ha! What is that doing on? Look! over on that TV is one of my favorite cartoons, Bugs Bunny! And That's the Happy Days Show! The Leave it to Beaver Show! The Carol Burnett Show! Land of The Lost?...I loved that Show! 90210?? Yikes! I laughingly thought. Wow! Look at that eighty's hair! I shouted as I pointed at the different screens.

What are all these TV Shows about? Why am I seeing them?" I wondered out loud.

Jesus answered, "They're memories...your memories. We are now entering the Artery of Memory. This is where you will literally see what lays in the walls of your own cellular memory. These images have been photographed and embedded on the walls of your cells. No worries though, I have gone before you to help change the scenery of what dominates your present reality. Keep walking."

"Ok, well that's good!" I said with relief thinking about the mullet I used to wear in the 80's. I was a bit cautious as to what else I would be seeing on the screens of my memory as we ascended the stairs. You never know at this point. I mean, I do realize He has washed me clean through forgiveness and mercy, but I was a bit perplexed as to why he was showing me all of these old images. What did they have to do with provision anyways? Hmm, interesting to say the least. But I knew Jesus enough to know that what he was allowing me to see was only for my own transformation.

We ascended a few more steps and I watched as the TV screens on the walls kept flashing from one show to another.

"That's the MASH Show! I remember watching that! Oh! That's the Andy Griffith Show! Batman and Robin! The Love Boat? Ha! Ha! Lost in Space? Oh, my goodness! Loved it!

Ohhhh, ouch! What is that? Oh no! That's the Carrie movie! Yikes! That was a scary one! Children of The Corn?? Oh my! ... Friday the 13th? Why?? Uh-oh! What are those movies doing on these screens?" I said with angst.

"Yes, they're all there aren't they? All of those shows you are

seeing have been lodged deep within the artery of your own memory." Jesus said.

I was kind of afraid to even look at him because I thought he might have a disgusting look on his face or something. But I couldn't help myself, so I looked up. To my surprise, but not really, I saw nothing but love and compassion in his eyes for me. My mind melted like butter once again at his overwhelming lovingkindness. Isn't it amazing how we view God in moments of vulnerability? Some people believe he is completely disgusted with us much of the time, while others think he is angry and just waiting to punish us. Then there are those who are spiritually awake enough to know the unlimited grace and mercy of God that causes them to fall more madly in love with him than ever before.

As I deeply pondered these things, a beautiful scent filled the air around me. I could feel mercy vibrating through my body. I don't know how I knew it was mercy, it just felt like it throughout my being. It's like I was smelling and feeling the aromatic wind of a tangible mercy and grace flowing over my skin and immersing into my spirit. It was wonderful and calming to my soul.

Jesus answered my thoughts again saying, "I am never angry with you, my friend. I am always for you no matter what. Why would I be angry with someone who is a part of me and so willing to absorb my way of love? I am here to help you live an abundant life, and that includes your thoughts; for that is where abundance begins. Your memories are just that, memories. You need not be afraid of the past or carry concern for the future.

I brought you here to help change what you were fixated on and to reveal what you were always meant to see. I don't control the remote control of your mind. It's your remote, it's your show. You are free to choose what goes into your eye gates. Our relationship is deepening, so what you used to like to watch has now changed into something different. It's not because you were afraid of what would happen if you chose to watch something powerfully influencing. But more because you are preferring the eternal experience of your understanding and to know someone else is intertwined in relationship with you. You are becoming more sensitive to the desires of your spirit over a sedative to your mind.

Another way to look at it is like sitting down to eat something. You're either going to eat something great or not so great. Great memories are built on great food. The smell, the taste, and the pleasure it gave you. And you also remember the time you ate something spoiled. It's the contrast between the two that causes you to know what you really do want and what you'd rather not experience again. But if you happen to stumble upon a few pieces of stale fish along your journey, you quickly remember what it tastes like just by smelling it. These are the subtleties and the "smellities" of life.

So, what channel would you like to watch now? I personally

like the travel and food channel's myself." Jesus said with a chuckle.

"Ha Ha! You are too funny! But what a relief for me to hear you say that! I was told I was going to hell for watching the discovery channel!" I said with a smirk.

"Umm, yeah, let's just leave that one right there, my friend. Keep discovering the heart of what is being revealed to you on this stairwell." Jesus said with compassion.

I took another step up the stairs and noticed another program playing that was so familiar to me in my youth. I pointed at the screen and started to laugh.

"Oh man! Look at that! The Jefferson's Show! "Moohoovin' on up! To the eastside, to a deluxe apartment in the sky! We finally got a piece of the pie! Ha ha!" That was such a catchy opening tune to the show! Such a funny series! I was always cheering the Jefferson's on!

Oh wow! Ok? Is that the Brady Bunch on that screen over there? So many of these old shows! It didn't really hit me as to just how many there were back when I was growing up.

Look! There's the Friends Show! And Seinfeld! And...oh no! another horror flick. Yeah, ok, moohoovin' on up the stairs now!

Oh! What's this! That screen is huge!

Looking over to my right I noticed a very large TV screen that looked to be at least 100 or 200 inches in diameter. It was blank with nothing showing on the screen.

"Oh! Now I see it! I know what that is! I love this music! Dunna dun dun dun dunna dun dun dun dunanu wamp wamp wa wa! That's the opening music for the Avengers movie! Yes! I love Marvel Movies! Wahooo!" I said with joy.

I was perhaps just a little too excited as I intently watched the screen. But I knew better than to get caught up in watching a mere movie, when I had the Creator of all Creators near me. My spirit was more than willing, but my flesh was a little weak with all of this imagery.

I took a peek out of the corner of my eye to where Jesus was standing. I was so curious to see if he liked the Avengers as much as I did.

"Yes! I like it too! Isn't this opening music composition just the best? When we were choosing the instruments to create the melody together it was so much fun." Jesus said with satisfaction.

"Wait! What? What do you mean when "we" were choosing the melody for the movie together? You mean, you helped the writers write that song?" I said with bewilderment.

"Well of course I did! Who else do you think helped them write it, the devil? Do you think the devil could write something that wonderful? Jesus said with laughter.

Ok??? Yeah, that's a grid blower right there. I didn't answer a word, because my mind was getting ready to pop off its hinges.

You see, this is where the memory of all my religious conditioning over the years gets in the way. On one hand, I know that powerful songs like the ones found in these types of movies could only come from another realm. They're not just your "typical" kind of composition that make you feel strong emotion. No, these are songs that move your very spirit.

Not everyone feels the same about these types of songs or compositions, and that's ok. I just know what moves the core of my being to want to live life to the fullest.

"Great movie eh?" Jesus asked with joy.

"Great movie? Yeah, awesome movie! I loved them all! The best part is they have helped me in several ways. I think it was the victory over evil plots and the "Anything is possible" parts I have come to enjoy so much. I could literally see how some of the elements in those movies could come true in the future. Is that right Jesus? I mean, who wouldn't want their own personal Iron Man suit to fly around in?" I said with elation.

"You are exactly right my friend. Movies like these unveil something in the heart of man that will be tangibly revealed in the future. We put them in movies, so people get used to what the future holds when they do become a reality.

"Meet George Jetson! ..Ha ha!" Jesus winked and laughed as he sung the opening tune from the famous Jetsons Cartoon Show that came out in the 1960's.

"I just love you Jesus! You're so much fun! It's like I've known you my entire human life! You're so comfortable to be around!" I said with overflowing joy.

"Well yes, that's because you have known me your whole life, duh!" Jesus said with laughter.

◆ ◆ ◆

Memories Old And New

We stood there laughing together singing all of the old show tunes until we ran out of breath. It was so healing and so much fun. It's difficult to describe the joy I was feeling and the love I was receiving in this moment.

After we calmed from the laughter I asked, "So why are some of these shows playing on the newer big screens, while others are playing on the older box TV screens?"

Jesus responded, "Some of the shows are faded memories of the past, while others are more recent memories. The small TVs represent the past and the large screens represent the present. They also relate to what dominates your thoughts. The big screen is more prominent in your thinking, while the smaller ones are distant memories. This is important to know because they reveal something about your life as a whole.

In other words, what you consistently think about becomes more like high-definition color to your present reality. The reason you like Marvel movies so much is because they speak to a part of you that bears witness to who you are in the earth. It's that part of you that lives in union with the inner you. It's the effortless flow you feel when you watch the movie play itself out in front of you.

In the same way, thoughts and emotion that match who you really are cause a magnetic pull to happen. It's the "Like attracts like" paradigm, where you start to believe this could really come to pass. So, tell me again how you feel when you hear the opening song of the movie?" Jesus asked.

"I feel like the sky is limitless! I feel like anything is possible! I feel like good is triumphing over evil! I feel like Thor striking his hammer down to deal with injustice! It feels so empowering!" I answered with boldness.

"Very good my friend! Those feelings are a direct reflection of what speaks to you the most. Everyone has those same kinds of feelings, only in different ways. Not everyone is as excited about Marvel movies or the Lost in Space Show as you are, but they are excited about other things that make them feel limitless. That's what makes humanity so unique and special. No one is left behind when it comes to believing the impossible, and actually, no one is ever "Lost in space". They just think they are sometimes." Jesus responded with a smile.

"But if I'm feeling this way, then why do I feel stuck? Why am I not there yet?" I asked.

"This is where it gets really easy. You are walking through the Artery of Memory. That's what these images represent, just memories. It's quite simple to change a memory by changing the channel. It may be a discipline at first, because your mind has been filled with resistance for so long, but once you engage things that are enjoyable to watch it gets easier.

If you don't want to watch Children of the Corn or Freddy Krueger type movies anymore then change the channel. Once you do, the weight of the old box TV will turn into a brand new Hi-def TV screen that is pleasing to the mind's eye. Magnetism then starts to pull the wonders of blessing towards you because you're now in a state of receiving, which is non-resistance. Where there was a challenge before in offering resistance to the unwanted imagery, now there is no longer a barrier or wall built up against the goodness that is trying to get to you." Jesus said with confidence.

"That is really good! Thank you, Jesus! It makes a lot of sense to me now. Especially the part about the resistance that causes good things to stay away from me. It reminds of the time I went fishing with my father-in-law Rich and his friend Bob. We were out in Bob's boat on the Columbia River in the Portland, Oregon area fishing for salmon. Anyone who has ever been out on a massive, fast moving river heading towards the ocean knows how dangerous it can be for boats trying to cross over into the sea. The force of the river rushing towards the incoming ocean tide causes a powerful turbulence and a downward current to occur. It's crucial for the driver of the boat to keep an accelerated speed in order to surpass the incoming force of the current. If the driver panics or dwells on thoughts about sinking to the bottom and drowning, then he or she may either turn the boat around out of fear or become paralyzed by the size of the waves he or she is about to engage. The key is to remain focused on the outcome of what you'll experience on the other side of the turbulence. I.e., The wide-open possibility of a great big ocean and the potential of netting a great catch."

I kept pondering this principle. It all seemed so easy, yet a little scary at the same time.

Jesus interjected...

"You were thinking all of that in just a few seconds? Wow! You do have an active mind! That is a great analogy my friend. I like it. But that tuna sandwich didn't fare too well in your stomach when you were bobbing back and forth on the river, now did it?" Jesus responded with a chuckle.

"Wow! You know about that? Of course, you do! I almost forgot for a second. Yeah, no, the sandwich didn't! But you certainly helped me through the "traumatic" experience with a whole lot of laughter to follow. Please remind me to never eat a tuna sandwich on a hot day while fishing! Ewww! Just the thought of it now makes me want to stop eating tuna for a while!" I said with a little disdain.

"That's why memories are so important eh?" Jesus said in a somewhat sarcastic tone.

"Yes, they most certainly are! I hadn't even thought about that incident until you mentioned it Jesus!" I said halfway laughing.

"I know! But that's precisely the point, so you could see the contrast of what you don't want and what you do want, the next time you step foot into a boat. You see, without contrast you wouldn't become acutely aware of the beauty you want to have in your life. It's like your analogy about flowing down river with the current in order to see the enormous blessing that awaits. The contrast is found in the opposite direction or the opposition of fear. Like you said, if the driver of the boat were to freeze or turn the boat around in fear to head upriver, then they would be going against the current of effortless flow and the ease of letting goodness take them to unlimited possibility.

◆ ◆ ◆

The Path Of Least Resistance

Everything flows downstream my friend. The reason people say things like, "It's all downhill from here!" or "It's an uphill battle!" is because it alludes to their belief that effortlessness doesn't exist. They've been so used to going against the current trying to paddle feverishly upstream with their toothpick-of-an-oar called striving. Humanity was always meant to go downstream without a paddle. That is your spiritual default of allowing. Keeping a set of oars in the boat for a safety backup plan is not the best idea. Throwing them out altogether is. In doing so, your effort will diminish, and my effortless acceleration will launch you thru the turbulent situation ahead.

This is how I could fall asleep in a boat in the middle of a major storm, and it's also why I could wait to move forward to help someone in need while walking the earth in human skin. I waited to intervene until I felt the non-resistant current of Spirit take me downstream in supernatural ability.

Sometimes people try to take you upstream where they live in the turbulence of survival-minded memories. They try to get you to see the "good" in hanging around the "Freddy Krueger's" in life in order to try and rescue them from their own turbulent behaviors. But until Freddy is willing to lose his claws by letting go of the death grip of his own resistant thoughts, then there isn't much anyone can do about it. The key is to wait until "Freddy" is genuinely tired of living life in a dark basement watching scary movies on an old box TV. Now, don't take me wrong here. I still love the "Freddy's" of the world; I'm just not going to enter into resistance with them. I will always reveal my goodness to all of humanity, but it's anyone's decision as to whether or not they want to keep the resistance active, and their claws raised." Jesus laughingly said while demonstrating the claw with his hand.

Watching Jesus form the "Freddy" claw made me think about how much I am not a Freddy movie fan and helps me to see what I don't want running around in my head! Dark, damp basements with abandoned furnaces are not something that appeal to me." I said with relief.

"Ok, are you ready to leave the claw marks behind to check out some more non-resistant scenery?" Jesus said with a deep breath.

"Yes, but can we wait just a second? This opening scene on the Avengers movie is great!"

"Whoa! Oh no!" As soon as I asked Jesus to wait a second, I slipped on the stair I was standing on. I fell straight down on my backside. Somehow the step became slippery while we were talking.

"Are you ok?" Jesus asked with concern.

"Yep, just fine!" I sparked with embarrassment.

"Ok good. You know, sometimes we can slip and fall for some of those memories...even the good ones. Come, follow me, and I'll show you something even better than those green-skinned superheroes!" Jesus said with care and excitement in his tone.

As I followed him up the remaining steps to walk out of the Artery of Memory, I felt guilty at the thought of even watching

a good memory to the point of hesitancy to his leading. How often have I camped on something I thought was so great that I chose not to reach for something better. As much as I love the hidden messages found in movies, what I longed for even more was to expand into the internal messages that Jesus was revealing.

I think I've been addicted to the thought of an abundant/adventurous life, but holding myself back from entering it all together. I just didn't know how to. I was always taught that it had to be hard to get something you wanted. I was told that I had to "Suffer to reign" in life. I wondered just how much of this was man's theology as compared to God's way for me. I was quickly discovering I had a lot of my own misunderstanding going on inside the mind-movies replaying in my own head.

Jesus answered my angst, "Hmm, "misunderstanding" eh? I'm glad you mentioned that word, my friend. Let's go to the next place I want to show you. It's called the Artery of Understanding."

As we made our way out of the Artery of Memory, I couldn't help but turn to look back at all those memories, both good and bad. You know, memories are a funny thing. They can hold us captive for years or they can be a launching pad of joy to create new ones. Have you ever met anyone who kept replaying old memories in their conversations with you? It's like they got stuck in some time period of their past. I don't know about you, but I've always been one to love new stories of faith, joy, and hope. Old stories merely keep the old memories active to the point of potentially causing someone to remain stagnant in their growth. There's nothing quite like creating new memories to keep things fresh and moving.

It's wasn't like Jesus was telling me not to cherish the good memories of the past. He was simply saying that he has so much more for me to experience in life.

CHAMBER 3

Enter the Artery of Understanding

A s we wound our way up through the remaining steps to engage the Artery of Understanding, I could feel the weight of what I was about to see. As we walked towards the opening, I thought about what Jesus said when it came to understanding and what it looked like in my own life. I couldn't help but feel a sense of excitement mixed with caution. I could sense the atmosphere shift as we walked in. With each step, my head started to feel disoriented, leaving me somewhat confused. It was kind of like the feeling you have when you first wake up from a deep sleep.

As we entered, I rubbed my eyes to focus and looked over to my left. To my surprise, I saw what looked to be like question marks written or etched into the "walls" of the opening of the artery. Surprisingly, the letters started to move. They made a loud cracking sound as they unseated themselves from the wall. It was so surreal. As they came off the wall, they started to surround us with dance-like motion. Some of them landed on me as if they were trying to communicate something. Intrigued, I tried to touch one, but as soon as I got close, it quickly vanished into thin air.

"What was that? Were those question marks alive?" I asked Jesus with somewhat of a shocked tone.

"Why yes, dear Watson, they most certainly are!" Jesus said

with a chuckle.

Ok, I knew another life lesson was about to come by the sound of that answer. If He is calling me "Watson", then we were about to go into some sort of a "Sherlock Holmes" kind of moment.

"Ok? So, what are those question marks about? Are they here for a specific reason?" I asked knowing they were for me by the obvious fact they landed right on my shirt.

"Why are you asking so many questions, my friend?" Jesus answered with laughter.

"Ha-ha very funny. Is that why they were floating around in front of my face? Huh? Is that why?" I said with sarcasm mixed with laughter.

"Actually, if you really want to know, they are there because we are entering the Artery of Understanding. It's the beginning point of wisdom and people have a lot of questions and trying to understand so many things. That's why you felt confusion in the atmosphere earlier as well. Come, follow me inside and I'll explain more." Jesus said with a skip in his step.

Hmmm…Ok, that makes more sense to me now, but I don't really like how this area feels, I thought as we walked through a somewhat smaller opening than the one in the Artery of Memory.

As we came through the doorway of the artery, it opened up to another massive area that went as far as the eye could see. It was like a wide-open expanse just suspended there in front of us. People were everywhere. It seemed like there were thousands, if not millions. I noticed they were all spread out, standing in "mid-air" conversing with one another underneath some sort of ledges or coverings positioned at various height levels. Some people were talking one on one, others were conversing in groups, and some were clearly debating over different topics. What did this mean? I thought. But before I could even ask out loud, Jesus answered.

◆ ◆ ◆

Hierarchy; Anchoring Under an Understanding

"Have a question?" He quipped with a smirk on his face. "I know you do and that's why we are here. I wanted to show you what humanity looks like when they stand under their own levels of understanding. The "coverings" or "ledges" you see over them represent their personal growth levels that come from train-ing, impartation, and conditioning. Notice how the coverings themselves are made of natural material? That's because some of them have been created out of a synthetic substance, while others are made out of wood and straw. It's important to notice that some of the coverings are sitting higher than the others be-cause they are competing for hierarchy."

As I listened intently to what Jesus was saying, I was amazed that he was unmoved by the fact believers were standing under a covering of their own making and choosing.

"Ok, now I have another question. If there is no such thing as competition and hierarchy in the Kingdom, then why do we see it everywhere in the Church?" I asked with a ton of curiosity. *(This is the one question that has always bothered me over the years. I couldn't wait to hear his answer.)*

Jesus responded, "I knew you would ask that too. Remember, we are viewing the heart of humanity according to free will. This is how I view mankind. It's much different than how man operates in society. They may have the mindset of hierarchy and build those types of communities according to their own choosing. But it's not the original "blueprint" of Eden had planned and it's not how I see creation. Granted, many do not know or under-stand the posture they've taken, but it doesn't change the truth of how I see them as equals growing in their understanding of who I am.

See those people sitting over there?" Jesus asked.

"Oh yes, over there to the right? They don't seem to have any coverings over them like the rest do. Why are they sitting down while everyone else is standing up?" I asked.

"That's because rest doesn't have a covering of understanding over it. They are sitting down because they've returned to the innocence of simplicity and they're enjoying the pleasure found in the finished work of who I am. I am love and love does not require understanding so much as it is a syncing into the rest of my good nature. The reason the others are still standing under a covering is simply a matter of perception and belief.

However, I don't fault anyone for not quite understanding something yet. My patience is endless, and my faith is sure; even when I know that some of them will take longer than their natural lifetime to experience freedom. They will always have eternity to grow and rest in me." Jesus said with joy as he took a purple glass marble out of his pocket and started playing with it.

I was speechless. So, this is what growth looks like through the eyes of love? Wow! I mean, my inner man knew this to be true, but to see it with my own eyes? Yeah, mind-blowing. I just had to know more.

"So, will you please share some more about the whole understanding and hierarchy thing with me?" I asked with an inquisitive tone.

"Of course! I love to help humanity see that it's not about hierarchy, but about authentic relationship. Man is certainly good at building pyramidal-type structures, but like many things, when man builds things in their own levels of understanding they will eventually become stuck. However, it is great to see them turn it all into something beautiful when it gets flipped upside down.

Pyramids are beautiful structures. They are wondrous to behold as they reach into the sky, but nothing compares to seeing one that's been spiritually inverted.

◆ ◆ ◆

Flipping The Pyramid

When a pyramid has been flipped onto its top, it becomes open and exposed with its V shape; kind of like two outstretched arms asking for help. A child raises their arms when they want to be picked up and held in their innocence. It's an example of child-like surrender rather than a closed-off pyramid of pride.

You see, hierarchy is man's attempt to gain a temporary sense

of security through their own efforts. They climb to reach for a power that is really just a mere illusion at the top of the summit. Have you ever noticed that the view from the top of a mountain is never-ending? There's always a higher one to see or another one to conquer. The grand illusion is thinking security, safety, and deep fulfillment are found through hard work that drove them to the top of the summit. It's man's attempt at reaching for something they feel will never come without sweat and struggle.

My question is, why not allow the view to come to you through non-resistant trust and play? In fact, I would say the view is already here! You can't go any higher than you already are. Humanity is seated with me in the heavens and some just don't realize that yet. This is the illusion of self-effort. Ego leads people to believe they need to climb, reach, sweat, and strive to reach the summit of a desire, when all that is needed is to let go and take the plunge into the wide-open expanse of playful oneness with me. It's where favor and every form of provision is magnetically drawn to match it.

In other words, all provision is looking for is its match. And Heavens match is found in heavenly places. That's why the invitation is always to "Come up higher!" Not in a hierarchal sense, but in a higher dimension of thought. This is why I could say to the blind man, "Receive your sight" and to the disciples, "Cast your net on the other side of the boat". The "Other side" is the opposite side of efforted ego, which is non-resistant thought. Once the resistance of self-effort is released, then magnetism begins to pull.

You simply cannot find that match with a hierarchy mentality. Hierarchy speaks ego's language because it spurs the climb through loss of identity, abandonment, neglect, and trauma. It feeds the desire to become something great in the eyes of man because it's driven to be noticed and loved. And when you've climbed that mountain a few times, the only thing left is an eventual inverted outcome. The "pyramid" then begins to reveal its scheme through an exhausted ego. Once this happens, the beauty of a surrendered inversion begins to be seen and heard in a way that values everyone.

That is why you witnessed the enormous diamond crashing into the sand on the beach a while ago. I wanted you to see the beauty of an inverted life and the radiance of its rainbow-colored spectrum flooding the earth. Notice how the "peak" of the diamond was driven into the earth so that all of humanity could see the rays of a surrendered inversion.

This is why I am ever reminding humanity of my love for them through the rainbow in the sky. It's a reminder of just how beautiful inverted lives can be. Rainbows are more than symbols of beauty, love, and mercy. They are also a reminder that it's not through hard work, and self-effort that you receive Heaven's provision.

There have been many people over the ages who believed there was real treasure at the ends of the rainbow, only to be left with disappointment trying to catch its trail. But if they had understood what I have been showing you, they would discover that opulent provision is revealed through the beauty of the surrender as they take it all in. The rainbow represents a supernaturally sign and wonder of effortless flow. When a rainbow appears in the sky, the only thing "necessary" is to simply take in its beauty. No one has ever really beheld a rainbow in the sky saying, "That's ugly" or "I bet that was a lot of hard work to create". No, quite the opposite. It's pleasant to the eyes for a reason and it shows up when there's an abundant supply of water nearby. And water is the substance that brings life to all things. It's the reflection of Spirit in nature that is effortlessly supplied.

Rainbows Don't Play The Hierarchy Game

Try applying the idea of hierarchy to the colors of a rainbow and see what you get. Every color is perfectly arranged and revealed in the covenant of the oneness it holds. No color is higher ranking than the other. Not one of them are competing for attention because they were birthed from the place of complete acceptance. They simply reflect the mercy of my goodness in their display. It's up to you how you receive the free abundance I am offering." Jesus said with a grin that lit up the entire artery.

"Wow! That was a lot to take in! I love rainbows! I enjoy looking at rainbows whenever they appear, but I especially love them in Hawaii, where they are plentiful. Thank you, Jesus, for that amazing explanation of hierarchy and the signs and wonder of a rainbow.

Pondering these truths, I thought about how people will chase after some kind of illusion in pursuit of gain. But at what cost? And if everyone I see here is standing at different growth levels, would it be safe to say that some of them may want to just stay in that level of understanding?" *(I asked these particular questions because I have always wanted to know why it's so easy for most of us to just settle where we are.)*

Seeing my dilemma of thought, Jesus responded, "It's easy to settle because it's familiar and many people adapt to what's already known and working. It's no different than living in a particular home where some of the things you have wanted are there and in working order, so why bother with the few things that need to be repaired or remodeled until later.

It's the same thing in a natural relationship. People settle all the time in the name of "core commonalities". If someone says they like a particular food that you like or you both have a common belief together, then that's good enough and they can just "work" on or put up with the rest that doesn't really align.

Ohhh, did I just say that word "work" again? Jesus said with a smirk on his face.

Oh, yes, you went there! I thought to myself as I pondered my own life. There's that "work" word again. It's funny that he mentioned the whole thing about how we believe growth involves work. But is that how nature really "works?" I mean, I haven't noticed the trees, the birds, and the bees running around shouting, "This is too hard! This is so much work! My wings hurt! My buzzer's worn out! My beak is broken! My limbs went limp! I can't stand change! I think I'll just settle right where I'm at and stop growing."

Can you imagine? The sound of all that complaining would be deafening, and we would most likely be left with a natural world full of miniature trees, wingless birds, and impotent bees.

"Yes, we most certainly would, wouldn't we?" Jesus said as he answered my thoughts. He continued, "All of humanity standing before us each have the opportunity to see growth as something effortlessly beautiful. However, not everyone is going to see it quite the same way because of their individual journey. This is the beauty of personal growth and free will. A person can either choose to remain dependent on the "comfort" of their own level of understanding or they can remain flexible to allow the undiscovered wonders of truth flood their hearts to expand their minds. Everyone wants to know truth, but the funny thing about truth to the intellectual mind is that it processes it like a math equation. Once they feel the equation has been answered they feel a security that leaves them content for a while. That contentment is called formula.

It doesn't mean they will not or cannot change eventually, but it does present the challenge of opposing viewpoints throughout humanity. This is where we can get stuck opposing the effortless flow of Spirit.

When it comes to differing beliefs about provision, this is an interesting one for sure, because it directly affects the belief one has in their current emotional state. Money is emotional to all who see it as their source of safety and well-being. And depending on what you believe about it will directly affect how your mind allows the receiving of it freely.

◆ ◆ ◆

Unblocking The Blockage

In other words, if a person has been raised to believe that

money is evil or difficult to get, then they have a "covering" or level of understanding over them that keeps them standing under lack. The poverty mindset can gain momentum in a hurry if we don't stop it with non-resistant thought. Once a person comes to the point where their negative momentum stops, then they become open enough to receive tangible awareness. Once awareness is received, then their covering of lack is lifted so that growth can move them to a higher level of understanding. Not from a mere intellectual one, but a heart-centered revelation. Once the heart searches it out that is when the mind begins to change. Once a mindset changes, then a synchronicity happens between the two. This is where the effortless flow of receiving starts to work in your favor.

You see, you cannot fully receive something if you have a disconnection or block between the heart and the mind. It's like the example of the broken veins you saw earlier in the Artery of Trust. People say to me all the time they have a hard time trusting their heart because their mind has convinced their heart to become disappointed or resentful through trauma and pain. But when the mind and heart become one through surrender back to me, a synchronicity happens. It's like a dam breaking open to allow the force of the flow to come through. This is what living in a non-resistant state is like. Things begin to accelerate and move quickly when the blockage is gone. The mind has now shifted into a downstream, receiving mode, breaking down the dam of resistance.

Ever notice that when you move into a posture of receiving the resistance of confusion and reasoning dissipates? In other words, double-mindedness loses its power to block what is trying to come to you. This is what your own understanding does to you when heart-faith is not allowed to affect the mind.

You've heard it said before, "In all of your getting get understanding" right? But what precedes the understanding is heart-trust. Without trust then the leaning on your own understanding keeps you standing under limited coverings for a while, perhaps even a lifetime. Once a person allows the covering of a particular belief to lift enough to receive more revelation, then what they've been asking for will in fact be revealed.

You can't really ask for something while standing in your "boat" of effort throwing an anchor of resistance overboard in the middle of a fast-moving river, while expecting to see the wonder of what is just around the next turn. That anchor will quickly turn into a millstone of intellectualism around your life if you're not careful. Your life then becomes a "drag" as they say. The only way to live an exciting, abundant life is to unhook the anchor of your own understanding and throw away your "oars" of self-effort to allow the pull of non-resistance to take you downstream. You don't need understanding when there's nothing but unconditional love drawing you into the adventure of abundant life and the element of surprise.

So, that's why you saw all those question marks floating around you. Are you "understanding" more now?" Jesus said with a twinkle in his eye.

"Umm, wow! Yes! I most certainly am, that's a lot to take in, but so many of those questions were answered too! I do have another question though! It's a big one!" I said with urgency. (As if I didn't have enough to process already by that huge download he just gave me).

Jesus laughed and said, "Ok, I "understand" go for it."

"Alright, so, if all of these people including myself, are "stand

ing" under our own levels of understanding, and some of us just won't budge while others are flexible to learn, then why do we feel the need to try and convince others around us to change?" I asked with heaviness.

"That is a very good question my friend. This is why I asked humanity things like, "Who are you to judge another man's servant?" And "Judge not lest you be judged with that same boomerang coming back upon your own life". You see, I really don't need anyone's help when it comes to growth. That is an inside job that belongs to infinite wisdom. I am the one who gives life and breath to every person, so why wouldn't I continue to help them mature throughout their lives? My mercy never fails. It's always in step with goodness following every individual the rest of their days. When a person is ready to change, they will slow down and turn inward to allow Spirit to reveal my guidance to them. Sometimes it's little steps and when they drive over a cliff in between? Well? That's what parachutes are for, or airbags are for, I should say. (*Jesus laughs*)

◆ ◆ ◆

Love Doesn't "Do", Love Is

But one thing is for sure, free will is the greatest gift I could give humanity. Why? Because it reveals a person's willingness to desire love. And love is who I am. This is why growing in understanding is left to the individual. If they want to discover more, it's there for the taking. If not? Well, that's free will too. That's also why I am not impatient with people. They can have just as much as they want or as little as they want. I don't get frustrated or upset either way. I love them just the same." Jesus said with a nurturing tone.

"But I thought you wanted your followers to go and preach the Gospel to all the world with plenty of money in their bank accounts? And go do the Great Commission without any lack in order to be a blessing to whoever they encounter? Isn't that what we are supposed to do?" I asked on the behalf of every Evangelical Christian who genuinely wants to know.

Jesus chuckled and said, "Now there's a whole lot of "doing" words in those questions my friend. Love doesn't do, Love is. This is why receiving is so important. Once you receive the wonder of who I am in this relationship, then the doing becomes a natural expression of love without any strings attached or ego to be satisfied. This is why the disciples could go from town to town without a money bag or lots of extra food in their "North Face backpacks". When love enters an atmosphere without any strings or resistance attached, provision automatically magnetizes itself to that love in such a way that meets the need in the moment.

Your only "job" if you want to call it that, is to live in that love wherever you find yourself along the journey. When you are expressing it in your own "level" of understanding, others who are in a similar growth level as you, will take notice and inquire. They will see how you are living your life and will be drawn to relationship.

◆ ◆ ◆

Living A Life Of Good News

Preaching the Gospel was never meant to become a professional "corporate" ideal or an occupation that profits off of others. "Preaching the Gospel" is simply living your life in union with me, and out of that union, others will see, hear, feel, and taste that I am good by the way you live.

When I mentioned to the disciples that I wanted to share many other truths with them, they were unable to receive at the time because of their own levels of understanding. What I was saying at the time was that I desired relationship, and as that relationship matures it reveals the "many other things". It takes time in the unfolding because free will was given.

In other words, I will share more "understanding" with anyone who doesn't want to stand under their own limitation anymore. Love has no limits nor time restraints and neither does relationship with love. The only thing "necessary" is to open the heart wide and receive like a child. When a person does, then provision comes right on time in a variety of ways. Once someone believes they are loved without any effort required, then there's nothing left but to receive. This is where the real adventure begins and where hierarchy ends.

> *"Once the pyramid mentality goes, then everything*
> *flows. Oneness is then revealed, and the soul is healed."*

Once the soul is cleared from limitation, then effortlessness begins to overtake a life. Isn't that good news my friend?"

"Yes! Yes! Yes!" I shouted with joy. "It's wonderful news! I don't want any limitations on my life! I don't want any covering that hinders me from discovering more of who I am or who you are!"

I could hardly breathe. I was overwhelmed with joy to the point of feeling like I would melt into a puddle of immense gratitude right in front of Jesus. Deep inside I just knew it was this good. I just knew it. But all of the conditioning I had received over the years had placed such limitations on my mind, causing me to believe something different.

My thoughts rushed with all of the zealous and immature statements I had said to people over the years to try and get them to change. If I'm being super honest, the truth was I wanted many of them to change because it made me feel better in some way. I wanted recognition for a job well done. Oh yes, I did want them to experience this infectious Good News the way I initially had, but I wanted them to experience it in my timing and my way. It was me needing to feed my spiritual ego. After all, I was merely doing what I was trained to do through religion.

I mean, let's get real. If you're not winning someone to Jesus every week as religion demands, then you're left to feel shamed in some way. I wasn't spiritually awake enough to realize people have their own journey to walk and was never
meant to look like anyone else's.

Sometimes it can take an entire lifetime for someone to see something we want them to see right this minute. I hadn't really thought about the whole "Free will" thing at the time. I just processed that as stubbornness or wrote it off as some "demon" trying to keep them from praying the "Sinner's prayer" with me. Yes, I do realize there could very well be some sort of blockage or dark hindrance there with that particular person. But ultimately, their free will is more powerful than any entity or limited understanding trying to deceive them.

◆ ◆ ◆

Free Will; The Evidence Of Love In Human Skin

The proof of that is the very fact that God made man after his own image. He gave man that ability before he ever experienced a fall. In fact, that is what Love does and who Love is. That is why free will can be so powerful and so painful at the same time.

But the beauty is when it's all said and done, love wins...always. That's why humanity keeps running back to Love in some form or another when life becomes too painful. Mothers know this all too well when their hurting child comes running home after a heartbreak of some kind. Love is inescapable and it is one with all of us. Some of us just don't quite have that awareness of it yet, because of the "covering" we are currently standing under. Unconditional love defies it all and leaves a person breathless wanting more. *(Stop for a moment and breathe that in my friend. Feel the bliss of this moment. Receive what Christ is giving you and allow your heart to expand beyond any limitation. He is waiting to take you on the adventure of a lifetime through limitless love.)*

◆ ◆ ◆

The Camp Called Choice

As I absorbed the massive revelation of what the Artery of Understanding meant to humanity, I couldn't help but notice the "encampments" or "shelters" that were spread throughout the artery. They looked like the campsites would you see in the woods or even those you would see amongst the homeless in major cities across America. It was odd to me because on one hand, we were in "Heaven" yet on the other, we were walking amongst the heart of humanity.

I asked Jesus, "Why are all these camps here? Do people actually live here?"

Jesus replied with a smile saying, "Paradigms! They are camped out here because their current paradigms and beliefs about who I am keep them from moving forward. Like I mentioned before, their understanding leaves them anchored like a tent peg driven into the soil of complacency. Without realizing it they've set up camp with a survival mindset that feels secure to their mind, but the truth is, it's an illusion of safety."

"An illusion of safety?" I sparked. "I thought that as long as they're in you then whatever happens from that point on is pretty much "your will" being done in their lives. At least that's what I was taught to believe. I mean, I know that people can still make choices and those choices have consequences, but ultimately it's all in you, right?"

Jesus answered, "You are seeing part of that right. Everything

and everyone has been created by me and through me, but not every choice has. That is left to free will to decide. Of course, all things work together for good, but sometimes people choose not to turn into that goodness. Love always presents a way of escape for my children, but it's up to them whether they want it or not. There is never a time when I don't have another choice available for someone. It's always there hovering like a beautiful hummingbird does in front of a flower. It's the free will to decide whether or not they choose to turn their attention towards it. Like the beautiful "bird" I'm always humming and hovering around your life with goodness. Remember, my friend, Goodness and Mercy are always following humanity whether they turn towards them or not.

The campsites you see are not evil in and of themselves, because they are all a part of the human experience. Some will camp on the revelation they've received and then pack up their site when they sense a prompting to receive more from me. Others will simply remain camped on what they've learned. They will drive their pegs down further into the soil of their own security every time the rush of my wind of change flows by. And they will once again repair the tears in their tent walls with the duct tape of their own self-effort whenever the "storm" passes. When they feel like it's too much to handle, they will then cry out to me and I will be their safety when their steel pegs of hardheaded understanding come loose. Eventually, they will get tired of living in complacency in order to embrace the change that causes them to surrender to their next level of understanding. For some, this is a weekend campout. For others, it is a semi-permanent base camp.

You see my friend, I am patient. I'm not looking for humanity to rush what doesn't feel like love to them. You can't hurry love and you can't force free will. Every single person on planet earth knows when change is upon them. They sense it, see it, and feel it, but they cannot escape it. Change is that one area of life that can feel like someone's whole world is coming apart, but once embraced something new emerges, giving them a brand-new start.

I will tell you this my friend, the longer a person remains in an encampment that was designed to be temporary, the more their surroundings begin to decay around them. Have you ever smelled the inside of a tent when a family has stayed in it for a week or longer? Yeah, well, we won't go there right now. You get my drift. *(Jesus turned toward me with a look of, "Ya know what I mean John?)*

Stagnancy and resistance are like blockages in the human artery or polyps in the GI Tract. They are bumps in the "road" of what was meant to be clear of obstruction. Remember what I said earlier, "It's all downhill from here". There's a reason life flows downstream. Life is supposed to have flow to it. Just like you were never meant to wear diapers forever, you were also never meant to live in a tent permanently.

My food is to do the will of Love and that food is always the freshest when it's harvested, eaten, and eliminated daily. Just as you cannot slice an apple open and expect its color to remain the same for long, so it is with the decision to mature in life. My desire is for all people to journey with me and sometimes it means breaking camp and moving at a moment's notice to engage with me in real time. Just because there is a suddenly in life doesn't mean Love is in a hurry. No, it could very well mean that someone needed to break camp due to their tendency to wax stagnant inside their own survival mentality.

My love is always flowing like a rushing river inside the veins

of humanity. I'm excited about my friends, and that excitement is reflected in the rush of blood pumping to and from the heart. Some people merely want to hang on and anchor into their own understanding, even in the midst of the rush of my love storm surrounding them. Rather than living the "let-go" life, they are too afraid of unconditional love that is constantly swirling around them. Others who know that understanding matures, embrace change because they know it is a part of life and a never-ending adventure of spiritual growth.

It's the same with provision. It's always there, but it takes letting go of survival in order to embrace the unseen realm of playful trust. Camping is supposed to be temporary and fun, but when you live inside the nylon walls of limited understanding, it can be a lifetime filled with stress and confusion. I just want my friends to enjoy life seeing the many sites and adventures along the journey, without the need to hold on to self-effort.

Life-Giving Food

Manna is an interesting food. It was given to my people long ago as a nutrient-rich substance that would last for the day, just like any other fresh food would do. It's light enough to flow through the human body quickly yet nourishing enough to sustain energy for the day. When I whispered the words, "Give us this day our daily bread" to the disciples, It was not only a spiritual example of how living in the present is where revelation is, but it is also a natural truth concerning food.

"Taking no thought for tomorrow" is simply living in my provision for the day in your mind. "Your life is like a vapor (Manna). Here today, gone tomorrow". I created each person to enjoy each moment to the fullest with me. What good does it do to eat ice cream tomorrow when it was meant to eat on a hot day today? Everyone knows what melted ice cream looks like when it has been left out on the sink for a day or two.

You see, understanding to the individual who is too afraid to change when I am revealing something new to them is like the person who misses the opportunity to experience a wonderful cruise to an exotic location. The cruise ship traveler is the one who took the risk to get on a ship they've never been on to go to a place they've never been to. When they return to tell the one who didn't go on the trip, they can only describe what it was like. It's a very limited view of what the trip entailed. It's not the same as actually being there. You have to experience it to know what it looked like, felt like, tasted like, and smelled like.

Now, it's ok if that person didn't want to go on the cruise this time around because eventually, they will go on some form of an adventure the next time around. It's inevitable. I have created the human experience with a built-in desire to explore the many facets of what life is all about. Even in the most challenging situations a person has faced in life, I have made a way for exploration. Even if they are the smallest of steps forward through a wave of emotion. Small steps are still movement, and motion was built into emotion.

> *"When babies take their first steps, they are unaware
> that giant leaps are an inevitable part of their future.
> They can try all they want to stop change from
> happening, but the eternal play found in internal
> adventure compels them to take the leap forward."*

What that means is eventually, most people cannot help but move from taking small steps that lead to bigger leaps of faith. However, if people still choose to live inside the toxicity of their own tent of limited understanding, I am still patient and kind with them. The Tree of Knowledge found in religion may not be patient, but I am.

I have brought you here my friend to not only see what the Artery of Understanding is like inside the heart of humanity, but to explain more of what it means from my perspective. I've made a way for all those who are stubbornly resistant through small "stints" of mercy that help to keep the artery from completely closing in on them. My love is eternal, and my patience goes far beyond what you've ever been told or shown by humanity. Now come, follow me to the next artery."

◆ ◆ ◆

Pondering My Own Campsites Along The Journey

I was floored by all the truth I just heard Jesus say to me. I can see why so many of us get stuck living inside of our own "campsite" dwelling on thoughts that keep us from living a life that is adventurous, and abundant. I understand now why humanity struggles to keep their stance under the covering of their own understanding. I've been there way too many times in my own life. I try not to think about it, but there have been so many times I have stood my ground on a truth to the point of making enemies I never intended to make. It wasn't that I had ill intent while camping out on a revelation of some kind. I just wanted people to be as passionate as I was about it. Unfortunately, sometimes that passion can be perceived as control, manipulation, and force. To be completely honest, perhaps there was some of all that in the mix.

Control is a funny thing, isn't it? We want to feel in "control" of something because we are afraid of not feeling we are in control. So, we fight for it in the name of truth and revelation. I can't tell you how many times I have witnessed this mindset on my own social media newsfeeds. Especially, around election time. People feel like they will lose more of their freedoms whenever a new leader comes into office, so they fight for their rights through words more than divinely inspired action.

A survival mentality will make people feel like their whole world is coming apart if they don't immediately spring into action trying to right a wrong. While this may be an honorable idea to some degree, there is always a level of understanding involved. And where there's levels there are coverings, and those coverings will always dictate an understanding of a truth and blind us from a greater one. Coverings and levels are why we have wars, racism, division, hatred, disputes, and disagreements.

Thankfully, humanity is beginning to awaken to oneness in ways that are indescribable. I truly believe we are now in a glorious moment of time where the saints of old could not have even imagined we would be in. God is helping us to awaken all by himself without the help of man. I am quickly discovering on my walk with him through the heart of humanity, that Jesus is more in love with us than we first knew.

You may have had the thought cross your mind, "Yes, I believe that too John! But what does this have to do with effortless provision?" It has everything to do with provision. Once a person is awakened to the truth about their own self-effort, they will never be the same. For it is in oneness with him that you find an effortlessness that has the power to create worlds. In fact, because of the oneness of Trinity; Father, Son, Holy Spirit, worlds are still be created by the unity of their life-giving words in the beginning, "Let there be light!".

Think of it this way. Have you ever watched a video of a huge magnet on a piece of machinery that comes close to a large piece of metal? Or have you ever used a magnet yourself to pull objects to it? I am sure you have in some form or another. If you have then you would know that the path between the two has to be clear in order for the connection to take place. And depending on the size of that magnet, it is almost impossible to pull two large pieces apart. In fact, in order to separate larger magnets, you would have to literally turn the magnets off or wedge something in between them to break the connection. *(Some pieces of equipment have the ability to choose that option, but most "regular" magnets don't have that ability.)*

Love is different. It's always magnetic and is constantly drawing every "willing" vessel towards it. It's the "like attracts like" analogy. In other words, when a person becomes that kind of love, they become one with the main source or the origin of its existence. It's the belief or level of understanding that causes many people to place wood, hay, and plastic objects around it to block the magnetism from working. The magnetism is still very much there and consistent with its own nature of attraction, but free will gets in the way of its pull.

This is what Jesus was meaning when he talked about the "tent pegs of understanding" holding the tents down in place. I knew with every fiber of my being this was the case in my own life. I knew this to be true with all of my efforts of wood, hay, and stubble when it came to money and provision in general.

Why was I so resistant to letting go of resistance when it came to provision? Why have I had such a difficult time trusting the goodness of God to simply provide for me without condition? It's not as if the God of love is demanding that humanity works for him in order to be provided for? The work scripture commonly quoted, "If you don't work you don't eat" didn't apply to Adam in Eden because he lived in innocence, and didn't know what work was before he fell into it through resistance. He wasn't engaged in anything but non-resistance. The ground yielded its strength to Adam because he was magnetized by pure love.

> *"When a person is the unadulterated "substance" of love they are a vessel of innocence. And when you are flooded with innocence, you become childlike, and when you think like a child, all you know is the wonder of play and the joy of receiving what has already been provided."*

As I followed Jesus into the next artery, I was feeling freer and freer through what he was revealing. Love is either big enough to slice through all of the seduction found in the Tree of Knowledge or it isn't. I was choosing to trust that he was more than big enough to awaken me to the fullness of love inside the Tree of Life as I walked and talked with him.

"Ok, are ready to stop thinking and start receiving more of what I am showing you?" Jesus said with a sparkling smile of all-knowingness.

He knew exactly what I was pondering on in my last few paragraphs and was "saving" me from going too deep with my own self-introspection. He knows us all too well, and he is the best at providing a way of escape from our own limited mindsets when we need it.

"Yes! I am ready to leave my current level of understanding Jesus!" I said with assurance. "Let's do this! I want to see what else is pegged down for me in the next artery!"

"Ha! Ha! That was funny John! "Pegged down" You did get your sense of humor from me, now didn't you!" Jesus said with the biggest smile I saw yet.

I was smiling as well, but I truly didn't want to see any more of those "tent pegs" that were driven into the soil of my own stubbornness.

"Alright! Here we go! Just around the next bend, you'll be able to see it. You're gonna love this! This is the one that gets me super excited. Well, they all do for a variety of reasons, but this one here…this artery makes my heart pump with excitement and joy for another reason. You ready?"

"Yes Jesus! I'm ready, I think." I said with a little reservation and a big gulp, knowing that each place had its own life lessons attached. I was truly excited, but it meant that I needed to let go of more resistance. Now, please don't misunderstand me here. I want to grow and embrace change, but there's a part of me that is still holding on because of past hurt.

Thankfully, it's dissipating, but I can still feel a piece of that tent peg stuck in my soul holding on like embedded shrapnel from former battles. Perhaps the next artery will be the one to

pull the rest of it out to fully release me.

I am trusting him more than ever before, because his nature is calming, and his smile is so reassuring.

CHAMBER 4

Enter the Artery of Creativity

"There! There it is! See it?" Jesus said with elation.

"OMG! Yes! Oh! Sorry Jesus! Didn't mean to say that!"

Jesus chuckled and said, "OMG! Is right! Over there is the Artery of Creativity! Isn't it breathtaking?"

"Wow! Wow! Wow! It's sooooo Wow!" I couldn't talk. What I saw flashing, swirling, rushing, gushing, and thundering before me was indescribable. The colors were unlike anything I had ever seen before on planet earth. They were mesmerizing and filled with life! What I was seeing was a torrent of swirling color before me. It was so brilliant, so beautiful, that it took my breath away. I wish I could describe what I was seeing accurately, but there are no earthly words for what I was beholding.

Just as I was about to pass out from the magnitude of the sight, Jesus reached over and held me up from crashing to the "floor" of the interior walls of the heart. I was struck speechless and felt like I had been hit with a million, tangible rainbows at once. It was intoxicating and exhilarating; like I had just been washed with the full force of Heaven's love.

"Yes, I know my friend. It's spectacular, isn't it? This never gets old to me. I love it more each time I breathe it in. Creativity is not just an action, it's who I am. I am the great I am in and through creativity. It's who I am to the cosmos and humanity. It cannot be separated from me. Come, let's walk over and take a closer look inside. I have much to show you." Jesus said as he helped to stabilize my wobbling knees.

◆ ◆ ◆

Intoxicated With Color

"Go in? We are going closer? How can I go any closer? Umm, I feel like, like, I'm going to burst!" I said with an intoxicated slur.

"You'll be just fine. I am with you. I will never leave you or forsake you to explode in the power of the color of provision. It may seem like you'll "burst" as you say, but this is where your mindset is fully exchanged for mine, and because it's an upgraded paradigm shift it feels like it will, but you won't wind up in a straitjacket, I promise." He laughed and then quickly turned to walk towards the entrance.

"Okay??? How am I supposed to take that?" I said under my breath as I followed him to the artery. I had already been feeling like I might "lose it" for years trying to "figure out" what this thing called provision was all about.

Knowing my thoughts, Jesus said, "That's just it my friend, there is nothing to "figure out". It's all about receiving and letting me do the "work" as you have fun creating for creating sake.

"What was that Jesus? Can you say that again please? I didn't quite hear what you said. Something about "work?" I couldn't hear what he was saying due to the volume of sound coming from the swirling colors in front of us.

Jesus stopped, turned towards me and said, "Try not to work your mind so much. Let's go to the next artery. I will answer more of your questions there".

"Ok? Sure. Will do! Mind! Stop thinking so much!" I muttered internally.

I wanted so badly to hear every word. I felt like I missed something he said only to be told he will answer more of my questions in a little while. I'll admit I was feeling somewhat impatient because I wanted in on every little nuance of what he was saying and doing in the moment. My mind was on overload. Jesus knew it and that's why he was smiling so much. Ugh! Nothing quite like your soul being confronted with the purity of unconditional love when you are feeling anxious and impatient. Again, I wasn't feeling any condemnation. It was more like, "I want to know everything now because I just can't get enough of you in my life experience."

As I followed him towards the entrance to the Artery of Creativity, I couldn't help but wonder what was next. This place, this artery, was unlike anything I was previously shown. I mean, they have all been spectacular in their own way, but this one was a mindblower. It seemed as big as a city or even a nation, and farther than the eye could see. It looked like there was no ending to the enormity of this place.

I kept thinking about the power and magnificence of color. Why does color have such an impact on us? It's so wonderfully pleasing to the eye, and healing to the soul, isn't it? As I continued to ponder, I began to notice something on the path ahead of us. Twenty feet or so in front of me Jesus was jumping up and down like he was earlier inside the Artery of Trust. Only this time something was splashing all around him. It looked like some kind of liquid substance from where I was standing. I couldn't quite make out what it was because of the many layers of color that now began to surround me as I walked closer to the entrance.

"What is that?" I thought to myself as I hurried my pace to catch up to him. "Wow! This is amazing! It's so, so..." I said with utter shock.

"So beautiful?" Jesus answered.

"Yes! Gorgeous! What is this?" I said with exceeding joy. Liquid colors mixed with crushed jewels were flooding the path all around us. They were not just "any" colors, these colors were from another realm. Never in my life have I beheld colors like these. There were blues, reds, a million different shades of indigo and purple, yellow, magenta, violet, white, green and so many other "cosmic" colors that were indescribable. There were flashes of color with iridescent-like glows to them, unlike anything I had ever seen before. What was so fascinating to me in the moment as I watched them flow around us was that they looked like they were alive; like they had personalities or something. I couldn't take my eyes off them.

"Aren't they wonderful?" Jesus blurted. He was smiling from ear to ear like a child on Christmas morning.

"Yes! This is the most amazing thing I have ever seen! What is this? What is happening?" I shouted with laughter.

Jesus responded, "They are the colors of creativity flowing out

of the image and inner core of humanity. They are the living colors of love that are individual and unique to each and every person. That is why you see colors you've never seen before on earth. There are trillions of colors here and yes, they are alive with vibrant personality and purpose. They are here to serve and escort us into the artery. They're excited to show us their home."

"Yes! Yes! Yes! I love that!" I blasted with thunderous joy. Somehow, I just knew in my heart this was absolutely true before he even said it. It's like the colors had already answered my questions as I beheld their excitement.

Jesus responded to my elation, "Yes, that's right! You know it because they bear witness with the substance you've been created with. Just like everyone else, you are made from creativity. You are created in the very image of creative flow. Love is filled with color and color is filled with love. You cannot separate the two because they are one, and love has many different facets to its nature when it's expressed.

Love is not an "it". Love is Spirit and Spirit expresses itself in many different shades of colors wrapped in human skin, and creation itself. I and My Father are one, just as the many colors of Spirit are one with you. We all reside within the make-up of who you are. Just as you cannot escape the colors of the world that surround you in the natural, so it is with the colors of creativity in and through the heart of humanity. Heaven is filled with color and this is just a small portion of what resides in the spirit realm. What is being revealed here is the invitation to see your journey and the world differently. The colors of my love are inviting you into their world of "Rose-colored" belief. It's one of your earthly slogans and it's true here as well. What does it mean to have "Rose-colored glasses on?" It means that you see things as they were meant to be seen...pure and good."

"Wow! Ok! So, is this why you created all the many different colors? I mean, you know, the colors we humans have to enjoy? Is it the main reason? To give us something different to focus on other than things that tend to be so "grey?" I said with a desperate tone.

"You are really close in your assessment, my dear friend, and even grey is a color, isn't it?" Jesus responded with a loving challenge in his voice.

Hmmm, why yes, it most certainly is a color, I thought. I now had so many more questions as images kept swirling in my mind about life on planet earth and why humans frequently focus on things that are so "grey".

As we stood there taking in this beautiful experience together, the colors began to move under our feet and lift us straight up off the "floor" of the heart to escort us into the Artery. It didn't feel scary, unstable, or awkward at all. It felt completely safe; like I could trust the colors with my life. It was like I had just been lifted up by trust itself or Jesus himself to carry me in. I didn't have a care in the world as we moved towards the opening.

As we moved forward, I could hear laughter all around us. It was the kind of laughter that makes you lose it with laughter. You know what I mean? …The laughing you may see on one of those funny baby videos circulating online.

The laughing got louder and louder as we moved closer to the entrance of the artery. "Jesus! Who is laughing? I love it!" I shouted.

Jesus shouted, "It's the sound of creativity! This is what pure creativity sounds like when its fully expressing itself!"

"What was that? I can't hear you too well with all of this laughter going on!" I shouted back as I doubled over laughing my head off. By now I was laughing so hard I thought I would wet myself, only I didn't need to worry about that because I was immersed in Spirit and didn't care.

"That's ok my friend! You don't need to hear what I said, just keep enjoying yourself" He slurred.

As we "pulled up" near the entrance I could barely breathe. I doubled over with laughter again as I watched Jesus roll back and forth in the colors laughing hysterically in front of the artery. He kept saying, "I can't stop laughing! Oh Lord! I can't! I just can't!"

The more he said it the more I lost it. Especially, when he said, "Oh Lord!". It was truly wonderful to watch. I wouldn't trade it for all the gold in the cosmos. This right here is why I live. If you've ever heard or witnessed Jesus laughing in the Spirit, you would know exactly what I am talking about. When you see or hear the God who created it all laughing and having a blast, it changes your entire life for the better. He never laughs at us; he simply loves laughing with us. That's the big difference between believing a shame-based religion over a genuine relationship with God.

When we both found enough strength to get up off the floor of color, I looked down at my skin and to my surprise, it changed. It was like all of those colors soaked right into my skin. It was mesmerizing. It kind of felt like I was in some sort of Avatar movie. Everything, I mean everything, was coated in a trillion different colors. Even Jesus was coated with it. I was stunned. I didn't have words to say. I felt like I just died and went to Heaven. It was beauty beyond words. Every imaginable kind of glitter and glow was shining out of our skin and flooding the atmosphere. Bursts of colorful light were shimmering, glowing, and shining. They were all dancing about our bodies like we were plugged into Heaven's electrical system.

"Jesus! What is happening?" I quirked.

"One second, let me gather myself here. Ok, now, are you ready for my answer?" Jesus said with intoxicating laughter. *(I could tell he was trying to regain his composure so he could answer.)*

"Alright, Ok I'm good now. Friend, what you see on your skin is creativity in all of its glory. I've opened your eyes to see what it's really like to become love from the inside out. This is how I see you and all of humanity. You are now seeing the same through my eyes. Life in the spirit realm is filled with color, laughter, and every imaginable and unimaginable part of provision's creativity, because it's sustained by and through love. It isn't based upon works, labor or toil. It all exists because of love.

When you mentioned the "grey" color earlier, that is the color of the in-between. The place of the veil. A veil of understanding that stands in between what's real versus the illusion of what humanity believes is true about the heavenly realm of provision. It's a smoke show, a smokescreen, laying in between the mind and spirit. It's no secret to all who know about me that the veil of separation has already been torn in two for accessing all that I am. The full manifestation of color has been waiting on the other side of it all along for whosoever will. It's the limited understanding of man that has kept them from seeing and accessing what is true."

Jesus stopped talking, stared at me intently with love pouring out of his eyes as bright and brilliant as the colors, and said, "Humanity as a whole believes that I require hard work and sacrifice in order to receive my provision. Yes, it's true that you exchange work for wages in the natural, because that is how your fallen earthly system operates. But not here. That is not how the spirit world functions. Let me ask you this; how hard do you think I worked to create color? Jesus asked with a serious tone.

"Umm, wow! Uh, I don't know the answer to that question. I want to say, you didn't, because you're God??" I said with insecurity.

"Great answer my friend! I knew you would say that, and I am so happy you are so inquisitive. But not just because I am God, but because unconditional love is effortless." Jesus said while trying to hold back his laughter.

Have you ever tried to hold back laughter when you were sharing something with someone, but you kept losing it because you got the "laughter bug?" It's not like you were being rude, it's just a real challenge to stop once you start. Yeah, that's what was happening with Jesus while he was sharing with me at the time. It was making me laugh as well while swallowing his healthy "doses" of truth.

"Come, I'll explain more as we explore the artery together." Jesus said with humor.

At this point it didn't really matter, I just loved being with him, watching him laugh. It was so intoxicating and fulfilling. I felt at home.

◆ ◆ ◆

The Orchestra Of Creativity

As we came closer to the main entrance, the laughter that was so loud and inebriating before, began to turn into the most beautiful music I have ever heard. It was as if the volume of all of that thunderous laughter in the color turned into Heaven's orchestra. The sound I was now hearing was so pleasing to my senses it felt like I was going to burst with ecstasy in the purest sense of the word. The music touched every sensory in my body and it felt like it was made just for me. The sounds were everything I loved in music and more. I was hearing violins, cellos, piano, flutes, trumpets, every make and style of guitar, chimes, bells, drums, synthesizers, clarinets, saxophones, and so many more that I didn't recognize on earth but were beautiful to the ear.

"Whoa! This music! I have never heard anything like this before Jesus! Please tell me more about what I'm hearing?" I said with wonder.

With each step we took, I heard more sounds that were unknown to me in the natural, but they were healing to my neurological system. They were so pure, and flawless in their composition.

Jesus answered, "The music you hear is the sound of creativity as its being played by each person as they engage the fullness of their own in and through full acceptance. With every person who chooses to embrace their colors of creativity in non-resistance, is when you hear something that affects you so deeply. We were both laughing hysterically a few minutes ago because we were feeling and hearing the sound of humanity engaging their own unique colors of creative flow in childlikeness. In other words, there is no compromise in the sound of pure creativity released from a place of joy.

In fact, when someone knows how much they are loved, and they hear the laughter of my joy over their creativity, that is when the entire cosmos begins to resound and reflect the glory of that color. What you are hearing is the sound of unified, effortless creativity exploding and exploring with playfulness. It's the orchestra of colors created by the desire of one's own heart. Didn't I say I would give anyone the desires of their own heart? I give it according to someone's will. If they choose to remain in the grey, then I still love them in their choice of free will. I will not and cannot force anyone to leave the grey to come into the full color they were created to be. On the other hand, once they choose to believe I am good and they hear the laughter of my love in the joy of those creating, they too can cross over to a life filled with the wonder of endless supply.

You are hearing instruments you've never heard before because they are only found in the fullness of playful creativity. In this place, you will find no resistance, strenuous effort, fear, doubt, questioning, sadness, anxiety, or insecurity. A surrendered return to the receiving of innocence will take you all the way in.

Remember when I held on to your arm to keep you from falling down when you heard the sound of swirling color? That was the strength of my joy holding you up because your limited understanding was making you weak. My desire is for every person to experience the fullness of creativity so they can embrace the full measure of color I have placed within them. As you are witnessing here, there is no shadow of turning on the colors or tainting of their expression. They are fully themselves, and because they are, the laughter and joy are so strong they overwhelm the body. It's the fullness of joy that brings inner strength to the creative flow of who I've called you and everyone else to be. Thus, revealing my goodness to humanity in such a way that causes them to want to know me. Once they know how much I love to laugh and create with them, provision is merely a byproduct of that joy.

You see, joy is actually an empowerment and technology that unlocks the entire "hard drive" of creativity. People just don't know how simple it is to rediscover their own vibrant palette of colors, because they get lost in the grey. Now, as I mentioned before, grey is still a color. Grey is the color that causes the hesitant one to want to eventually engage the full spectrum of my goodness.

> *"Grey skies were never meant to keep the blue from shining through forever. Blue skies are ever-present because they don't lay underneath a level of understanding. Their only "covering" is the limitless creativity of love."*

Just as you cannot take the blue out of the sky or the emerald green from the ocean, you cannot remove joy from creativity. They are always there, and they are eternally reflective of my goodness. Come, let's continue on." Jesus said with glee.

◆ ◆ ◆

The Secrets Of Friends

Wow! Wow! Wow! I was truly dumbfounded by all he unveiled. I mean, it's one thing to read about God's goodness, but it's something far different when you experience it coming from his own mouth. My heart was pounding with love for him. I just can't get enough of this amazing God.

Aren't you glad he calls us friends instead of servants? Jesus himself said it in scripture and therein lays the difficulty for anyone who still believes they are in service to him more than they are in friendship with him. This is why he keeps calling me "friend" as I walk and talk with him throughout this encounter. He is reminding me that servants don't receive secrets, friends do.

"Do you want in on another little secret?" Jesus asked as I stood there in awe at all that was swirling around me.

"Yes! Of course!" I said with joy.

"The music you are hearing, the color you see, and the unexplainable joy you are feeling, are all a part of who you are, just as much as they are of me. You cannot separate color, music, beauty, wonder, excitement, joy, elation, laughter, creating, and flow, from Love. You're made of these things because you are one with me. I want you to feel what you are feeling in this very moment, all the time." Jesus explained with excitement in his voice.

"Yes! My spirit knows this is true! But why does my mind have a difficult time accepting this truth sometimes? Why is it that I do so well for a season and then other times I crash and burn feeling shame, inadequacy, and unworthiness? Have I been trained to believe I must suffer in order to reign in these areas? It all seems so foolish to me now, but I still struggle with the thoughts sometimes". I responded with noticeable frustration.

"I completely understand my friend, and that's why I wanted to show you firsthand what limitless love and creativity looks, sounds, and feels like. I want you to experience what life is like in oneness with me. This is what life is for me every moment and it is available for anyone who chooses to believe it as well. You are struggling with a "bi-polar" dis-ease called dualism and doublemindedness. It's not like you have a real disease or anything, so relax (he smiles). What you are wrestling with is the efforted highs and lows of thinking one minute you are deserving of good things and the next believing you have to earn them through suffering and unworthiness. This kind of thinking has to do with the conditioning you've received over the years, due to the skewed doctrines and perceptions of me.

It's kind of like when you walk into a candle store or a coffee shop and hang out for a while. When you walk out of one of those places the aroma stays with you for a time. It's the same with cigarette smoke, alcohol, wood fires, and a health spa at a resort. Some of these scents linger longer than others do. Sort of like survival. It tends to hang around for a bit longer permeating your outlook.

But did you notice that in all of these "aromatic" scenarios they do not define who you are? No, they are mere smokescreens designed to distract for a time. Eventually, they wear off and you go back to being your own unique "scent" again.

Where it gets a little "smelly" is when a person swallows the grey "pill" and remains complacent living in a tent with a level of limited understanding.

This is why I constantly remind the spiritual elite and the egoically-religious leader about who they really are. Everyone has the ability to climb to the top of any corporate ladder or religious mountain peak because they are the very essence of creativity, curiosity, and determination. But sometimes that curiosity not only has the ability to smell up the cat but kill it. And when that "cat" has had enough, it will either come to the point of surrendering to maturing in love or it will find itself in a difficult position high up in the Tree of Knowledge, with nowhere to go but down, a long way down. This is where spiritual leaders of all kinds begin to fall into depression, anger, frustration, and even suicide. *(Jesus hung his head and paused for a moment choking back tears of great compassion for all who have been trapped in a never-*

ending cycle of torment, with seemingly no way out).

I tell you this truth my friend, no one needs to go through mental torment believing I am requiring them to suffer for me. My heart aches for everyone to see what you are seeing right now with me. I want everyone to experience the fullness of color. If they only knew just how much I want them to be happy, joyful, and creative, without any strings attached, they too would be laughing hysterically at all the lies they were made to believe.

I am the Tree of Life, and anyone who chooses to abide in me will feast on the wondrous fruit of limitless creativity. The Artery of Creativity represents what union looks like. Oneness and unity to me look a whole lot like what you see here. If I were to meet face to face with every single person on planet earth and tell them they have full permission to be creative, to laugh hysterically, and to enjoy play, do you think they would take me up on it?" Jesus said with a raised eyebrow.

"Are you asking me Jesus?" I asked with a puzzled look.

Smiling, Jesus responded, "Yes, I am asking you."

"Uh, well, I'm not so sure if they would? Because it seems that you have already given them permission to do those things?". I responded with more of a question in my tone.

"Exactly! Yes, now you are seeing it. You are seeing it because you are standing directly inside of creative flow. Permission to create is always granted. It never shuts off. I designed the arteries to be a reminder of what my heart is always saying. Life-giving blood pumps through every human heart, and with every beat, I am giving it.

When I spoke the words, "Let there be light!" It wasn't a temporary decree. I was creating a sustaining and lasting environment within the cosmos that would not only be a reminder of my nature but an ongoing momentum that keeps the light shining and the colors swirling.

In other words, everyone has a built-in reminder inside their own heart that says they are creative. It's a choice to decide if they will ignore that light by shutting off the music and suppressing their laughter or engage the energy of eternal creativity. You see, self-pity and unworthiness are the lies that keep people reaching for the grey paint to "grey wash" everything in sight. But what happens when a colorful personality walks into the room to greet them? Now, depending on what shade of grey the one being greeted is in, will determine how they will receive that color. The vibrant color will either remind them of who they really are and awaken them with joy or they will become resentful towards it. Jesus said with a love in his tone that flooded the entire heart of humanity.

I could feel his heartbeat from where I was standing. With every beat the artery began to respond in unison, splashing vibrant color high into the "air" like a volcanic eruption. As the color plumed, I looked back down at my skin and noticed it was pulsating in unison as well. It was as if the myriad of color was feeling his great love towards humanity and responding with passion. I don't think any living person has ever really felt the full measure of his colors before. I was only feeling a fraction of them and it felt like I was going to explode into a pool of color every time I beheld them.

I could only imagine what it would be like if every person were to embrace the full measure of creative flow in union with Christ. OMG! Wow! What would that look like if we all received and activated it and then began to walk it out in alignment with our true identity? What a colorful world we would have! Just imagine if every bit of the "grey" in life were to be swallowed up by the vast colors of his love? I know it's coming because there's a place called home in the center of everyone's heart and all of humanity is being called to run back to it. They are starting to hear the sound of their own Eden again and they are discovering for themselves the permission to be who they were born to be.

"Home is where the heart is. Creativity is where
you can experience the vibrancy of life hearing
the sound of welcoming laughter coming straight
out of the heart of a creative God."

"Great thoughts my friend! Couldn't have said it better myself" Jesus said with resolve. He continued, "Just as I would never chastise or correct a child from creating, I would never hinder an adult from rediscovering the wonder of the colors of their own creative flow. Now let's go see what else this glorious artery beholds, shall we?" (*He said that as if he didn't already know what was inside. Hmm, what did he really mean by that? I wondered.*)

"Ah yes, glad to answer that question too. The thing about creativity is that it's always creating in the now, otherwise you wouldn't see such brilliance. Yes, every person can create and has in fact created their own "color-filled" past, but to live in the present now where I choose to reside, causes the color to remain alive with well-being and adventurous fun! Try telling a child to live in their past when they have a hundred crayons and endless paper sitting in front of them. Notice how they will grab the crayons and start coloring something in the present while you are still talking about the past. The only time they might draw something from their past is because of the conditioning of an adult's covering over them that has limited understanding attached to it.

"Reminding someone of their past when they want
to abide in the now, is like offering them a box full of
grey crayons. There are just too many colorful options
waiting to be accessed in the variety of the present."

I am the breath of inspiration that is always present. Therefore, I am living in the moment of color with you. Love is present and because I am, I find my joy in watching you explore creativity as it's happening. Does that answer your question? If not, no worries, I am quite sure you will see what I am talking about in a moment." Jesus said with that wonderful smile on his beautiful face.

"Yes, ok, it does answer my question in more ways than one!" I said with even more questions flooding my mind. I felt like I was on brain overload, yet inside I felt fully alive. His answer is reminding me of all the times I have been reminded to remain present, and to stay out of the future and the past. It's not like I've forgotten what scripture says about anxiety, worry, fear or even concern over provision. I mean, how could I ever question all of this provision? It's all right here and it's more than I could have imagined! It's all true, but why do I still question it sometimes?" I said with my mind wanting more answers.

◆ ◆ ◆

A Peculiar, Familiar Prompting

As I was trying to process all I was experiencing, I felt a tap on my ankle. I looked down and to my surprise, I saw a small "swirl-like" being filled with colors dancing around my ankle and waving at me trying to get my attention. It was so cute I could hardly stand it. I just kept staring at it. But the more I stared the more it kept waving at me with urgency. It really wanted to show me something. I looked up to see what it was trying to show me, but the waves of color were swirling and crashing around the main entrance like a roaring, turbulent waterfall. I looked over at Jesus to see if he wanted me to follow the little guy, but he was already walking straight through the "curtain" of liquid color ahead of me. *(The rushing, roaring, swirling colors surrounding the entrance looked like a huge curtain-like waterfall. The area surrounding the main entryway to the Artery of Creativity was so big and so vast that it was hard to tell when you were actually entering it. I thought we were already inside, but we were only just beginning to enter.)*

"Ok, it looks like we're going in! Let's do this lil' Swirly!" I said to the colorful little guy waving me forward.

As I followed "Swirly" and Jesus into the roaring liquid curtain of color in front of me, I couldn't help but feel like I was in some kind of a Narnia or Avatar movie. Here I am following Jesus and a little human-like ball of swirling color into an artery called Creativity. Yep! Just what I thought was going to happen when I met Jesus long ago! Yeah right! I've witnessed some pretty awesome things in my life, but this certainly tops it all. At this point, nothing is off the table with my journey. I've learned that although my spirit is already "there" my mind will eventually catch up to this. Yes, it may need a few more "colonics" but it is detoxing as I speak. "Right now, I just need to stay in receive mode, right Swirly?" I looked down at him waiting for an answer, but it seemed he didn't verbally communicate, yet he appeared to understand what I was saying and just kept waving me forward.

Ok, "I'm right behind you lil' Swirlster."

Moving forward, Swirly disappeared into the massive wall of swirling color. At first, I was thinking the sheer velocity of the swirl would spin me around like an oversized washing machine, but it didn't.

"Ok! Well? Here we go!" I said with courage.

As I walked through the otherworldly waterfall of rushing color, it was like all of my senses lit up into a full array of ecstasy and pure elation. It felt like I had literally just stepped into the throne room of Heaven. The only way I can describe it is like being turned inside out and I was now wearing my spirit like a "west suit" on the outside of my body. It felt powerful, wonderful, and exhilarating, yet supernaturally natural. Like I was finally the real me without limitation. So much so, that my mind was being saturated to the point I was now starting to fully agree with it.

In through the wall, I went. With each step, I could feel my entire body being "supercharged" with a purpose, brilliance, and overwhelming joy that was beyond my own. The colors of creativity were saturating me from head to toe as I moved through. Kind of like a carwash would do to a car, only way more colorful and saturated all the way through. *(I don't know why, but I started thinking about how much I enjoy driving my car through the car wash back home. I thought, "Yeah, those rainbow-colored streams of soap inside the car wash don't have anything on this!")*

I began laughing again at the thought of it. The more I laughed, the more the colors responded with exuberant energy. It was as if the colors were cheering me on and encouraging me to keep laughing. I guess this is what real "medicine" feels like. I wanted to stay there forever. It was that wonderful. I don't know how long I had been inside the massive opening, because the depth of the wall or curtain was as "thick" as the length of a football field. Time seemed to slow inside this huge portal of color. As I slowly inched my way forward with ecstatic bliss, I heard a loud splash in front of me. It was Jesus poking his head back through the colors. Just his head was poking through the hole he made with his face. He said, "Are you coming? I know it's the greatest "bubble bath" you've ever experienced, but it's time to show you more."

"Yes! I'm coming. I'll be right there. I, I, will be there in just a second." I said with intoxication. I was completely relaxed and feeling really good at this point; like I just had the massage of a lifetime followed by a spa treatment that made you turn into a puddle of relaxation. My body felt like pure honey ready to spread onto a delicious piece of toast. I had "died' and gone to Heaven, or had I? I was so blissed out that I couldn't even think straight with my natural mind. My words were slurring, and my body wasn't helping me too much when it came to moving my legs forward with urgency.

I slurred, "Swirly! Where are you? Swirlster! Are you still there?" I was wondering what happened to my little "friend". I could feel myself taking another step and then I heard a loud...

"Slap!"

Just like that, the colors around me stopped splashing and fell to the "floor" with a thunderous clap. I sobered a little and thought, "Whoa! What happened? Why did it all just stop?"

I looked in front of me and then down towards my feet at the feel of a familiar tug. It was Swirly waving me forward again. I asked him, "Why did it all stop so suddenly? Oh yeah, I forgot you don't speak, you just wave."

The color surrounding the artery was still there as far as I could tell, but something happened to cause it all to cease. Is it because I made it through to the other side? What is happening right now?" I asked myself.

I was still sobering up coming out of the powerful experience.

When my eyes cleared, I found myself standing inside of what looked to be like a tropical paradise.

"Now wait a minute! I thought I was standing inside the Artery of Creativity? This looks like Hawaii or something! How could this be an artery?" I was puzzled as to how I could one minute be entering a part of the heart that was filled with color, yet now be standing in a tropical scene.

As I took in the magnitude of the beautiful scenery all around me wondering what just happened, something caught my attention. Suddenly my eyes were drawn to my right and I saw Jesus off in the distance. I had to squint to try and see what he was doing, but I couldn't quite make out what it was. I could tell there was a lot of movement where he was standing in the midst of all the colors rushing, swishing and swirling all around him. It looked like he was standing high up on top of something. I couldn't make out what it was, so I followed "Swirly" over to get a closer look, and with the hope that Jesus would explain why the curtain of roaring color crashed to the floor around me.

Swirly ran out ahead of me and disappeared into the color close to where Jesus was standing. As I followed him closer, I couldn't believe my eyes. Well, yes, I could believe my spiritual eyes, but my natural eyes were going, "Huh?" Could it really be? Nah! Is it really? I thought with pure excitement. Yes! It was Jesus on a surfboard! He was surfing on a wave of color on the side of the artery wall!

◆ ◆ ◆

The Maverick Wave Of Limitless Possibility

"Come on in! The water's fine!" Jesus shouted above the roaring color. He was riding an enormous wave; like the ones you would see in wintertime on the North Shore of Oahu, Hawaii or the area called Jaws on Maui. The wave was beautifully intimidating. It was a mountain of color cascading down the side with thunder-like ease.

"Wow! Ok? I would love to join you, but I don't know how to surf a massive wave! You're the Pro! I'll just watch you from here!" I said with hesitancy.

"It's ok! Come on in! You'll know exactly what to do once you dive in! Trust me! You're a maverick wave surfer and you just don't know it yet. Oh! And by the way, the reason the swirling curtain of color crashed to the floor, was because the colors were finished transforming you to the point of seeing through a new paradigm. From this point on, you will see creativity as an adventure of your own making. You are the one who created this tropical paradise of a reality, just by thought alone." Jesus said with assurance.

"Wow! Ok! I like that! I like that a lot! I do feel "charged up" and ready to create some more! Ok! Here we go!" I jumped into the wave with every ounce of courage I could muster in the moment. To be honest, I had mixed emotion going on. I loved the idea I could create anything with my mind, but at the same time, I was intimidated by the size of the wave that stood before me. But I knew that if Jesus said I could ride it, then I could do it.

"Splash! Pop! Whoa! Yes! Ok, Let's do this!" I said with laughter and awe.

Out of nowhere a surfboard popped up underneath me and lifted me out of the colorful "water" and onto the wave. It felt like a perfect fit. Like I had been surfing my entire life on a board that was well-worn to my own grip and perfectly molded to my body. It literally felt like a glove that was tailored made just for me. The board began to take me right up the back of the wave and drop me right down next to Jesus.

He was right. I was a big wave surfer and didn't even know it. My feet felt like they were at home on top of the board. It was effortless and fun. We surfed that wave for what seemed to be an eternity carving it up together, surfing the barrel, and doing backflips off the top of the wave to catch another one. It seemed like nothing was impossible as we rode side by side laughing our heads off together. I was surfing on "top of the world" next to

Jesus having the time of my life.

Then suddenly Jesus stopped carving and leaned his surfboard towards me on the crest of the wave. He stood there on top of his board hovering in place, looking from side to side at all the wonder and beauty of what the artery represented. He had the biggest grin on his face as if to say, I am so pleased with what I created. It was a moment I'll never forget as I hovered there next to him on my board. I closed my eyes to feel his presence and this mind-blowing experience of a lifetime.

Suddenly the sound of the wave underneath our boards went from a thunderous roar to a calming stream of bliss. I began hearing the same kind of music as I heard before entering the artery. It was the sound of a mighty orchestra playing a beautiful ballad. As I listened, the tangible fragrance of plumeria, citrus, and what seemed to be like fresh rain danced across my senses, causing life to flood my neurological system. It was healing to my once, fear-filled nerves.

Again, I asked myself, "Is this Heaven? Is this what Heaven is really like? If so, I can't wait to be here forever."

As I absorbed the beautiful music and fragrance surrounding me, I heard Jesus whisper, "Yes, this is Heaven. The Heaven that has always been dwelling on the inside of you. Isn't it wonderful? This, my friend, is your very own creative nature we are experiencing together. I am having so much fun I can hardly stand it.

Whoa! Ha! Ha!" Splash!

Jesus fell off his board and sunk into the wave. I opened my eyes and looked over to see what happened. Surprisingly, his board was still "riding" in the same position, but he was gone.

"Whoa! What happened? Where are you Jesus?" I said with a little concern.

"Smack!"

Jesus came flying out of the "water" and landed on top of his board just as quickly as I asked where he went.

"That was awesome! It was true! I can hardly stand it I'm having so much fun!" Jesus said with hysterical laughter.

"Ha! Ha! Ha!" I started laughing with him to the point I almost

fell off mine as well. We laughed and laughed together for the longest time. Wave after wave of joy hit us like it did before we entered the artery. I couldn't stop laughing and neither could he. We were caught up in the ecstatic joy of the moment together. "I never want this to end!" I shouted with passion. "Neither do I!" Jesus responded in like tone.

I can't tell you just how healing this moment was for me. It's hard to explain really, but all I know is this is what pure love and acceptance feels like. Jesus was genuinely loving every second of his time with me. There was no trace of obligation, duty, or toleration in his demeanor towards me. He was in love with who I am.

Trust me dear reader, that alone is enough to make you want to be one with him for eternity. Nothing, and I mean nothing, compares to seeing and hearing Jesus having the time of his life with you.

"Ok! That was a blast!" Jesus said as he brushed off the excess "water" from his shorts.

I thought, "Now why would he need to brush the colored "water" off of his shorts? It's not like we were in a regular ocean or anything."

As I watched him brush the "water" from his shorts and body I heard a loud splat on his board. "Is that? Yes! It's Swirly!" I said with excitement. Jesus brushed Swirly off of his skin as he was wiping down. Wow! Swirly just manifested straight off of the color-filled skin of Jesus!

I started laughing again at the sight of this lil' guy. It seemed he was excited to see me too! He started laughing as he stood at the end of Jesus's board. He was slapping his hands to his "knees" while bending over belly laughing as he watched me laugh. It was the greatest thing to watch. Jesus was laughing too at the "cuteness" of this lil' guy I call "Swirly".

As we all stood and laughed together for a while, Swirly then jumped over to the front of my board, turned, and pointed forward. He was still laughing, but he was waving us forward as if to say, "This is the way! Let's go!".

"Isn't 'Swirly' as you say, just the best?" Jesus asked.

"Yes! He is so cool! He reminds me of a little swirling, ball of color that looks like the baby "Groot" on the Guardians of the Galaxy movie" I said with a smile, but then caught myself getting nervous about the mention of the Galaxy movie to Jesus.

"Ha! Ha! Yes, he sort of does doesn't he? Yeah, it was my idea for the movie. I snuck a little clue in the script for the purpose of getting people to think about a character who doesn't talk much but points the way for his friends. Notice how Groot is a root of what looks like a tree? Yeah, that's a clue as to what a living, moving, speechless thought looks like as it prompts people to movement." Jesus said with a smirk.

"Wait! Wuuuut? You gave that idea for the movie? Wow! Now I've just about heard it all! Please tell me more about this little "Swirly" guy here. You really have my attention now! I was wondering why this lil' fella was tugging on my leg and then waving me forward." I said with a longing to know what this meant.

"Ok, let me "color" the picture for you. Ha! Ha!" Jesus answered with laughter. "Swirly is not a 'he' exactly, and its name is Prompting. It is neither male nor female. The reason is because not everyone can handle or relate to the voice of a male or a female in the moment I am prompting them. Prompting is whatever it needs to be for the individual to move forward at that time. Notice how Prompting is made of color? That's because color does not have a specific gender, rather it's all things to all people. One individual can gravitate towards a certain color while the other is drawn towards a different one. That is why Prompting is multi-colored. It doesn't make a difference what color people feel drawn to in the moment, because I want them to feel peace and safety each time they sense my Prompting. It is there to help guide them when it's time to take a step.

You get excited when it appears because you already have a knowing that it is safe to follow my Prompting. But it's yours just as much as it's mine. We are joint heirs of all things, remember? So, you can call it Swirly if you want to. Personally, I think it's a cool name." Jesus said with love flooding his tone.

"Man! Ok! Wow! That makes so much sense to me now! Thank you for telling me that! I knew there had to be more to the "Swirly" story!" I said with awe.

"Oh yes, there's quite a bit more. Want to hear?" Jesus asked.

"Yes! Of course. Please do!" I responded.

"For the sake of our conversation I will call it Swirly too (Jesus smiled). I will also refer to him as a male since that is how you currently relate to him. Is that ok with you?" Jesus asked.

"For sure! I like it! I love it! Great!" I responded with joy.

"Ok, so, Swirly showed up along your journey when we were approaching the Artery of Creativity. He didn't show up before then because you were not at a level of understanding where you were ready to fully receive Prompting in the way he showed up here. In other words, Swirly is fully received when a person has let go of resistance enough to sense and acknowledge the subtleness of his prompting. It's not as if he hasn't always been there.

No, it has more to do with the eyes of your understanding being opened through awareness to see he is there to help you. It can only happen when you are in a restful place to receive the colorful guidance and safety of Swirly's nudging.

Once a person moves past their own survival levels of understanding to embrace the reality of Swirly's leading, that is when they have engaged my mind. And the mind of Christ is the very essence of playful creativity. You see, love in its purist form is the definition of creativity. The proof of that is when someone falls in love. Not only can you not stop thinking or talking about one another, but you also dream the wildest dreams together. In that state of mind nothing is impossible for either one of you.

It's the same way when a person walks through the journey of trust to enter the heart of Eden. Once they know they're home they feel safe. Once they feel safe then old paradigms and memories are purged to the point of seeing. Once they see what I am doing, then they are flooded with the joy that leads to creativity. For some it's a much faster process of awakening, but for all the others? Well, it takes a while and that's ok. Swirly is always there to remind them to take another step. Some people are only able to feel it while others are able to see it and feel it. Either way Prompting or "Swirly" is always there colorfully pointing the way." Jesus said with a dance.

"Wow! I love that! Having eyes to see and ears to hear comes to all who are ready for it, right? I asked.

"Yes, when they are ready for it Prompting is always there as an

internal guidance system to help lead the way. I am all things to all people. Swirly knows how to guide someone with joy, because he is the very essence of creativity in "prompt" form. In other words, when I prompt someone to follow through with something, Swirly is the safe and joyful feeling a person senses when I am leading. Peace is the tangible substance for the mind that is one with mine. And when the mind trusts enough in its safe home, creativity then reveals itself in a way that draws them into productivity that is void of effort.

Isn't this fun? It's so effortless, isn't it?" Jesus said as he busted out a few dance moves on top of the surfboard.

By now I had completely forgotten we were even surfing! That's how much I was caught up in the moment of hearing about Swirly, and the awakening I was experiencing with every word Jesus spoke.

As I watched Jesus lean hard to the right on his surfboard to carve up more waves, I was completely awestruck at the revelation and wonder of it all. I couldn't help but feel like I was having the time of my life as I stood atop the surfboard of creative flow. I mean, you would think your legs would give out from "balancing" on it for so long, but it wasn't like that at all. I was standing in oneness with Heaven's creativity and because I was, anything was possible.

Because I've always honored big waves and surfers in general, that desire led me straight into the center of an encounter with Jesus on a surfboard riding a maverick wave. Swirly was also there to help guide me when I was feeling a bit apprehensive about moving forward. He was and is the color-filled joy of hope and reassurance that leads us to those things we've only dreamed of.

My smile must have been as big as the wave as I watched Swirly dancing around on the tip of the surfboard. It seemed he was having the time of his lil' life as well. I was so caught up and mesmerized at the sight of a tangible expression of the Prompting of Jesus dance his little heart out that I didn't notice Jesus circle back towards me on his board. Can it any better than this? I thought.

"Yes, it can, and it does!" Jesus shouted as he lunged straight out of the water underneath me and grabbed hold of my surfboard.

"Ready or not! Here we go!" He shouted as he pulled down on the right side of my surfboard.

"Splash!"

Both Swirly and I fell into the ocean of color and sank underneath the surface, laughing all the way down. I opened my eyes under the surface and saw Jesus treading water there waiting for me. I started laughing again when I saw Swirly swim over to hop onto his shoulder. They both waved me forward as I soon realized holding my breath wasn't necessary in this artery either. I had an instant reminder that trust was my oxygen here too inside the Artery of Creativity. In fact, everywhere we went in the heart of humanity oxygen took on a whole new reality for me. The oxygen of love was all the grace and mercy I needed to breathe. Love filled my lungs with the "air" I needed to trust my way through the arteries on my way home to Eden, and now it is creativity that is painting them with the pure oxygen of joy as I engage the play of creative flow.

I could feel the colors painting my insides as I breathed in and out. Liquid love was covering my internal organs. It was like the best massage you've ever had, only from the inside out. The joy I was feeling was hard to describe. I just kept lunging backward and forward over and over again laughing hysterically under the surface of the "ocean". It was like I was getting tickled in the stomach over and over again. I couldn't stop and didn't want to. Creativity was overtaking me, and I loved every second of it.

I don't know how long I was enjoying the ecstasy, but it must have been more than a minute, because I could feel that familiar Swirly tug on my ankle again. As soon as I felt his touch, the "tickling" in my stomach began to subside enough to follow the lil' guy forward. As we swam back towards Jesus, *(who was by now several hundred feet ahead of us in the ocean of color)*, I couldn't help but think about this overwhelming feeling I have had since before I entered the Artery. It has been nothing but pure fun, joy, excitement, energy, and flow. I was not only having more fun than I've ever had, but the energy! Man! The energy I was feeling was electric! Like I'd been plugged into a major power grid of glorious, love or something. It's the most wonderful feeling in the world! Is this what it feels like to be fully alive? To be entirely and completely spirit? I wondered as I effortlessly glided toward Jesus.

Jesus was now standing on the ocean "floor" on top of something that looked familiar to me, but I couldn't quite make out what it was amongst all of the swirling color surrounding him. As I floated closer the colors "cleared" and to my amazement it looked like the same kind of jewels we encountered before, or at least it seemed like they were. Jesus was standing on top of an endless mountain of gemstones, gold coins, bars, and every other glittering jewel imaginable. They were strikingly beautiful, with mesmerizing rays that shot outward to what seemed to be a few hundred feet or more in every direction.

Wow! I thought the first pile of gemstones was mind-blowing!

Wow! Wow! Wow! But this was like an entirely different layout of gemstones under the sea! I was so filled with awe that I shouted, "This is the Crystal Sea, isn't it? Is this the same Crystal Sea as the one we "swam" in before?"

"You are indeed a smart one Dr. Watson!" Jesus laughing said as he fell backwards into the pile of jewels and disappeared.

"Ha! Ha! No way! I mean, yes way! The colorful sea is filled with millions of gemstones of all shapes, sizes and colors! I thought it was called the "Crystal" Sea because it was clear, you know like "crystal" clear? I asked with utter amazement.

"Splash!"

Jesus broke through the surface of the gemstones and answered, "It's colorfully clear! Because the light of my presence is shining through the gemstones. And what happens when light hits a jewel? You got it! Color! The Crystal Sea is actually a clear reflection of my multi-colored nature."

Jesus then disappeared back under the mountain of jewels.

"Wait! Please tell me more!" I said laughing at the way he would disappear into the jewels and then pop back up to say something. He was like a kid in a candy store. Or at least it seemed that way, only one of those gemstones could buy an entire one!

"Splash!"

Jesus broke through the jewels again saying, "I am the Light of the world, and because I am in you and you are in me inside the heart of humanity, that light is something that cannot be hidden. The jewels represent the endless provision that comes from being a light, the light of creativity. Notice how the gemstones are sitting underneath the surface of creative flow? That's because they are the bedrock of provision. When creativity is expressed through playfulness provision surfaces as the biproduct.

◆ ◆ ◆

Everyone Has Creativity Living In Their Spirit

In other words, when a person gets lost in the fun of creative flow it gives the gemstones or "provision" buoyancy to come to the surface. The opposite happens when a person doesn't feel worthy enough or forces creativity to produce something solely on a survival/need-driven basis. Therefore, keeping most of this provision held down and hidden.

Another way to look at it is like this...Now, I know it may be a bit of a challenge to do right now with all of this beauty in front of you but close your eyes and picture a snow globe in your mind. You know, like one of those fun little decorations you have sitting in your house around Christmas time? It's like having one of those snow globes sitting on your shelf and never picking it up to shake it in anticipation of seeing the snowstorm. The decoration was never meant to simply sit on a shelf without seeing what it was actually designed for. The snow-like substance begins to lift to fill the "sea" inside of the glass dome, the moment you move it.

It's the same with creativity. Leave it on the shelf without

"stirring" it up, and you'll never see the wonder of what your very own hands can do. Remember, it was you who decided to choose faith to jump on to the surfboard to ride the waves of reality with me. It was Swirly who kept reminding you it was safe and fun to engage what your spirit always knew to be true about you. And notice what happened when you got lost in the creative bliss of it all? You had no thought of how you were going to pay your bills or where you were going to get your next paycheck from. You were lost in the play of life in union with me.

Again, remember provision doesn't come just because you created something. Its buoyancy happens when the magnetism of play has drawn it to the surface. The joy that is found in and through play, is the strength of weightless magnetism that draws all good things to those who find themselves in light-heartedness and joyful creativity. The fortified wall of resistant worry that builds to keep provision out, cannot remain standing in the presence of fun that is fully engaged.

That is why I said that life intertwined with me brings fullness of joy, and abundant provision. The way to enter fullness is the willingness to let go of all the good intentions found in the baggage of self-effort, to embrace the ease of my provision.

You, my friend, had the courage to enter the heart to engage the artery because the weight of your own striving became too much to bear. And it certainly helped when you saw what was behind curtain "Number 1" back on the beach. LOL!" Jesus laughed as he sat cross-legged playing with the gemstones on top of the shimmering mountain of wealth.

"You know, there's nothing quite like having fun no matter where you are." Jesus said as he tossed another jewel down into the "valley" of the seafloor.

"No matter where you are?" I asked

"Yes, no matter where you find yourself along the journey. Haven't you been having fun since we started this adventure together?" He asked.

"Of course, I have! I'm having a blast here with you now! But, if I'm being completely honest, my journey before this hasn't always been that fun" I said with sobriety.

"Well, could it be that you didn't understand then what you now know to be true?" Jesus replied.

"Yes, but it seems I've wasted so much time not having fun and being so serious. I guess it's the way I've been conditioned. I thought it's how you wanted me to be in a world that is seriously messed up! But watching you this entire time has convinced me things don't always have to be that serious, and I should be having a lot more fun. I mean, I did struggle a few times as we walked through the arteries together, but I realize now that much of that was just my own paradigm. I want to have more fun! I want to be more like you Jesus!" I said with excitement.

"Ok, well? Then stop being so serious." Jesus said with a smile as he slid down the pile of gemstones and out of sight.

"Alright? Ok? That's easy for him to say. I have things like bills to pay, responsibilities, and well? Serious things to deal with! He's God! He can have anything he wants!" I mumbled under my breath as I looked over at Swirly to try and get some sympathy. But he wasn't buying it. He just floated there staring and blinking at me, as if to say, "Really? Jesus just told you to stop being so serious, are ready to stop being serious? We have more "funning" to do." He didn't say it with words, but his stare said it all.

My heart sank, and I knew Jesus was right. All of my serious-ness was actually causing a lot of resistance in my life. It's no wonder greater levels of provision have eluded me much of the time. I'm finding that the "weightier" matters in life are those found in joy. For in joy is found much strength." *(Hmmm, that kind of sounded a little like a Yoda quote there...lol.)*

Swirly raised his hand and gave me that familiar little wave to follow him.

You know what I'm finding interesting about myself as I'm watching all of this wondrous opulence unfold in front of me? Is that my mind has been programmed to automatically default to a mixture of doubleminded questioning. One minute I'm having a blast with Jesus knowing this is all true, and the next I'm doubting this is all real. "Oh, the wretched man that I am sometimes, eh Paul? Is that kind of what you meant about your own life?" I thought to myself as I followed Swirly.

"Woosh!"

A loud swishing sound came up behind me. It was Jesus flying through the water like Aquaman thundering through at warp speed. He flew right by me as if there were some kind of emergency he needed to get to in a hurry. The color-filled water rushed by rolling over me like a tornado ripping through a field. The force of the water threw me into a turbulent summersault like a surfer tumbling underneath of a huge wave.

"Swish! Swoosh! Girgle!" Around and around, I tumbled. "Whoa! Ohhhh! Whoa! Whoa! Ha! Ha!" I shouted as I thrashed around in the sea.

Laughter filled my mouth as I rolled around in the turbulence. It felt like I was being cleansed in a huge washing machine. It was wonderful yet a little intimidating. But with every tumble, I could sense the colors speaking to me. No, they didn't have an actual voice per say, but I could feel their frequency speaking to me through the motion I was experiencing. Their voice felt like imputed wisdom. I just had a knowing what they were conveying to me in the moment.

It's not like Jesus wasn't trying to throw me into some kind of harmful tailspin when he flew by me in the water. No, this was meant to happen for a reason. I could feel my mind being renewed and transformed as wave after wave rolled over me. The strong current was taking me where I could not take myself. I was at the mercy of the colors.

I just kept thinking, "Allow this to happen, because it was meant to happen John. Let the colors take you where they want to take you, they are safe. You can trust them." With every pull, roll, and rush over my body I could feel myself trusting the creative flow of the moment. The water saturated my mind, spirit, soul, and body. I felt a rush of creative power blast through my veins with every tumble. It's difficult to fully explain, but I was becoming creativity.

◆ ◆ ◆

Jesus "Blooping" Around

Just when I had reached the "climax" of the experience, all of the sudden the water began to calm around me. The thunderous rush became a slow, soothing flow surrounding my body. "Wow! This feels so good!" I thought. "I feel like I've just been made new. I am new! Something is different! I've changed!" I said out loud.

I could now feel the fresh current of color begin to move me in one direction. At this point, I was completely relaxed. I was putty in the "hands" of the water. My mind was no longer questioning what this meant. I had just been infused with a divine contentment that no longer needed to know. I was entirely satisfied with all that was and is. It was something I had never experienced before. Not at this level. This was Heaven's bliss flooding through my entire body. I was now given over to the fullness of creativity.

"Bloop! Bloop! Bloop!"

What's that? I said to myself. I heard bubbles "popping" in my left ear. It was a little funny sounding. It made me think of a goldfish blowing bubbles in a tank or something. I opened my eyes to see what it was, and it was Jesus hovering near my ear mouthing the words, "Bloop! Bloop! Bloop!

You thought I was a fish, didn't you? Come on! You know you did!" He said with belly laughter.

Laughing, I said, "You got me! Yeah, I kinda did think it was a goldfish or something. I never know with you Jesus!"

"How did that feel?" Jesus asked.

"What? The Blooping? Or the washing?" I said with a smirk.

"No, the recalibrating! The reuniting! The reminding! You know, the swishing, and the swooshing experience you just went through?" Jesus said.

"Oh yes! The recalibrating! The reminding! That is exactly what it felt like! I just didn't have words for what happened. It was amazing! It felt like I just came home from a long journey to experience a rejuvenating spa-like therapy treatment. I didn't know it could go that deep into my soul! I didn't realize just how much it felt like home to give in to my authentic nature. It's like I have always been one with it. Is it me? Or a part of me? I can't tell!" I asked with wonder.

"Yes! It's a big yes to both!" Jesus replied.

His appearance quickly turned from being "stained" with color to completely saturated in it. He looked as if he became one with the colors around him. He disappeared for a moment and then returned. I could see the outline of his body for a moment through the thick colors of the sea when he returned. Then he would disappear again into the colors of the sea around us. He did this for several minutes as I watched with amazement.

"Bloop! I'm back!" I heard as he appeared right in front me. It startled me for a second, but in a good way. I started laughing at all of his "blooping" around.

Jesus continued, "This is what it's like when you sync into the real you that's always been here. You see, Swirly led you by my love to engage this experience in a such way that felt completely safe for you. Some people have a very difficult time embracing the oneness of who they are if they don't feel secure enough with my smile of approval. If they even see it at all. In other words, if they live in opposition to what is truly effortless, then there's a block in the flow. If humanity only knew just how much I approve of the creativity they are one with, then the earth would be filled with it. Darkness would be replaced with an array of color so bright it would light up the entire earth.

It's not only my desire for them, but it's also the very reason they are having their human experience. Creativity is the direct byproduct of knowing and experiencing my love and acceptance. And creativity is the revealing of just how much love exists and how real I am. Some realize it, but far too many believe that creativeness is something for someone else and not for them. They are challenged because they don't see the joy of who I am and the fun I am having through its flow. They see the opposite much of the time.

Think about it. If all you know is a false image of love, then all you would experience is the effort of surviving. If that's the case, then why would you even need or want to look to a God who you feel doesn't approve of creative flow?

This is why it was important that I led you to this place through the Artery of Trust. To remind you of the life-giving tree you were hewn from and the one that is always waiting for you to come and play. You see my friend; a safe home is where inspiration is revealed. Once it's known, then safety is the atmosphere in which fun is fully experienced. Once fun is embraced then there's an unconditional invitation to align with your authentic expression. Once it's released, then the state of bliss you experience in that flow keeps you in childlike play. And when you remain in the power of play mentally and physically throughout each day, that is when payday comes in a variety of ways.

That is why you see me having so much fun with you. I want to not only remind you of who you are, but I want you to experience the full permission I've given you to explore your authenticity. I approve of you no matter what, but I have fun with you when you believe I really do approve of your own creativeness. To prove this, I gave you an imagination to create with. That's how much I support your creative ability."

"Bloop! Bloop! Bloop!"

(A puffer-like fish appeared in front of me and started changing colors. It was funny looking. It had big, human-like lips and eyes as big as an owl. I started laughing at the sight of it because it was just like Jesus to "blow" it up with creative imagination right in front of me.)

"I see that! I feel it! I really do! I have been completely consumed with joy watching you play this entire time! You are the one who led me here. You are the very source behind this genius display. I can literally feel how much I have changed since I followed you on the beach through the first entrance. It felt like I went from striving to an effortless state of being. It's all so fulfilling! Will I remain in this mindset or will I soon forget? I don't want to doubt it, but the world around me is so filled with stress, frustration, anger, hard work, and striving. I want to be the color of well-being they need!" I said with passion.

"This experience is very real my friend. It's my nature within you. That is why I chose to take you on a spiritual journey of the heart. This is how I see you and everyone else. It's a journey of awakening, revelation, and transformation. But the way in is to fully know that I am the source of all life within and around you. That means love is the very oxygen that is not only sustaining you but is you. This is far different than living by a set of rules and protocols that were developed by humanity in order to feel a sense of security. It's really just an illusion and distraction from all that I offer as true safety.

After the fall of man, I watched as humanity tried to find their way back home through the Tree of Knowledge. Because I gave man the free will to explore, they fell for the seduction of independence trying to care for themselves in the wilderness of their own understanding. This is where self-effort becomes their motto, causing them to believe that hard work is the way. Sometimes this kind of sweat and toil does work, but at what price? You see, effort beckons a person to give it their all with the hope of a pay off in the end. Sometimes it does in fact pay off, but at what cost?

◆ ◆ ◆

When Is Effort Ever Enough?

Effort rushes through the raging rivers of society shouting, "Keep paddling! Keep working! You're almost there!" But little do they realize there is never a place called "there". Humanity is an eternal species with no ending. Eternity is always here in the present now and never in an illusionary place called "there". In other words, tomorrow will be another now. That is why I say things like, "Take no thought for tomorrow". Why? Because if you're living in the present, then you won't be thinking about a place called "there" tomorrow.

The Tree of Knowledge will have people paddling up a creek until they eventually lose the paddle through fatigue. Once the paddle is gone, the downstream flow of the current takes you right into living in the now where effortlessness is always present.

> *"Effort is an unending call for humanity to continually dine on its fruit. It's a never-ending cycle of striving versus the refreshing flow of inspiration."*

Let me ask you a few questions my friend. How difficult was it for you to have a joyful conversation with me back on the beach? How challenging was it for you to receive the gold bar or the wad of cash when I tossed it to you? How painful was it for you to let go of your fear to fly down the slide with me? How hard was it for you to let go of your own fear of past memories as I comforted you in the Artery of Memory? And how difficult was it for you to let go of your own effort to embrace the living colors of the turbulent waters, just a few minutes ago?

Now, before you answer any one of those questions, think about what this entire experience with me has meant to you in light of your religious conditioning? Do you see how difficult life is, trying to maintain survival?" Jesus asked with pulsating love.

"Wow! I am completely in awe of what you've been revealing to me! How did I ever survive before? How in the world did I ever make it? Why did I buy into the lie that life had to be so hard? Time with you is nothing but easy!" I said with breathless relief.

"I did say my yoke is easy and my burden is light, didn't I?" Jesus said with a chuckle.

"Yes, you most certainly did! But now I see more of what you really meant by that statement. I had no idea until now! I can see what you were saying by being with you this whole time!" I exclaimed.

"Wahoo!" Jesus shouted, and then slid backwards down the mountain of shimmering jewels and disappeared.

I started laughing again at the sight of Jesus plunging into the mountain of gemstones. It was the most beautiful thing to watch. To see the Creator of it all having so much fun with his creation changed everything for me. I never fully understood that God is not only the originator of fun, but he loves to have fun with us. I was mainly told that to be a Christian or a Christ follower, life had to be mixed with suffering, hardship, hard work, seriousness, and perhaps a sprinkle of joy now and then as a reward.

◆ ◆ ◆

The Purple Stone Of Creativity

I mean, after all, there are far too many serious things going on in the world today John, and if you have too much fun, people won't take you seriously! I said to myself as I watched Jesus swim in and out of the jewels laughing uncontrollably.

"Swirly, catch!" Jesus shouted.

I looked over and saw Jesus holding a large, purple-colored gemstone in his right hand. He was getting ready to throw it over to Swirly who was now swimming up behind me. Jesus wound up his arm like a baseball player and pitched the gem over to him.

"Swoosh!"

I felt the gemstone thunder past me in the water and smack Swirly's hands. Amazingly Swirly caught it with ease and started dancing around cheering like he had just caught the fly ball of a lifetime. He then wound up his pitch and threw it back over to Jesus.

"Smack!"

The jewel hit his hand. Jesus laughed and said, "Get ready my friend, here it comes!" As he looked over my way.

"Swoosh!"

I could hear it spinning through the water towards me, only this time the gem started to glow. So much so, I could hardly see it as it smacked my hands. It burst into what seemed to be a million little jewels of every size, shape, and color.

"Wow! So beautiful! What is happening?" I said to myself.

Jesus answered my thoughts, "Ha! Ha! What you see are millions of gemstones that represent millions of creative ideas inside the heart of humanity. The purple gemstone I threw to you represents the royalty of creativity, that will release others to engage ideas, inventions, and technology in every way imaginable. Not just to engage the ideas, but to receive an effortless mindset that allows them to manifest these things for the well-being of humanity.

You have become one with my heart and I have given you full permission to journey to the center of creativity with me. When effort is relinquished in the soul and mind, nothing shall be impossible for you. Endless ideas and heart-centered solutions for humanity will continually flow to all who embrace the journey to end their own effort from life lived in the Tree of Knowledge.

I am The Tree of Life that brings healing to the nations. It's now time for creativity to reveal itself through all who embrace the ease of my nature. I love you with a never-ending kindness. Now go and be the effortless provision I have already provided to all who will receive." Jesus stood there on the glistening mountaintop of gemstones looking at me for what seemed to be an eternity as he said those words.

My heart exploded into a million pieces of love for him. I started laughing and crying all over again at the thought of how much this generous God loves me. My eyes gushed with gratefulness under the Crystal Sea. Imagine that!

As I continued to pour out my love for him, Jesus waved, turned, and disappeared into a swirl of color.

"Swoosh!"

Swirly followed in his own "Swirly fashion" waving and dancing through the water with ease. He stopped just short of where Jesus was, turned back towards me and waved me forward. As I followed after them, I heard a heavenly, melodic sound behind me that was beautiful to my ears. It sounded like a symphony of a thousand chimes converging together. I turned around to see what this was.

To my amazement, it was the sound of jewels coming together to form the one purple gemstone again. There was a magnetic pull that caused all of the other gemstones laying on the sea floor to follow suit. As the last one filed its way into the purple gemstone, the purple jewel started to glow so bright that it lit up the entire sea with many different shades of purple, indigo,

amethyst, orchid, iris, periwinkle, violet, lavender, and mauve.

The glowing gemstone then moved toward me and started to speak. It was a familiar voice. It was the voice of Jesus! He said, "I am with you always. Love is the substance of provision that comes in unexpected and unusual ways. You would do well not to try and figure it out or expect it to show up in a way that will cause you to trust in your own self-effort again. Be the reflection of love's royalty wherever you go, and I will surely be with you.

> *"For when you become one with the dance*
> *of inspiration, you will find me and endless*
> *creativity in the center of it all."*

◆ ◆ ◆

Shot To The Heart

"Woosh! Smack!"

The gemstone then thrust itself into the center of my chest. It felt like I was hit with the power from Heaven itself. I could feel the jewel begin to separate into a million gemstones inside of me like it did just moments before in the sea. It felt glorious! It felt wonderfully beautiful! It's like my entire DNA had just changed into something entirely new. I could feel creativity rush through my veins like a blood transfusion from Heaven. Wave after wave of color flooded my entire being to the point I knew that I knew I was made to create.

From head-to-toe, brilliant ideas and witty inventions from Heaven infused my very being. It seemed that every solution that mankind needed, instantly rushed through the swirling colors to saturate my mind, heart, and internal organs. They were pulsating through my veins. So much so my mind could hardly handle it.

When the power of the experience began to subside, I noticed that I was being carried by the flow of this new infusion. Like a newborn child being carried in his mother's arms. I was totally at rest. It was no longer me telling my body to move. It was the current of love carrying me. I felt completely at peace inside as I began to flow towards Jesus. Is this the peace Jesus was talking about when he said to his disciples, "Peace I leave with you. My peace I give you, not as the world gives I give you?" I thought as I melted into his embrace. It felt like a tremendous gift.

Have you ever been so saturated with peace and approval that you literally felt like your own body was 100% spirit? This is what it felt like and then some. It was literally like I lost my outer shell of a body and became born again into a whole new reality. I felt one with everything around me. The colors of the sea, the jewels, the arteries, the heart, and Eden.

As the current of creativity carried me deeper into the artery, I was now internally transformed to take in every little nuance of what was being shown to me. It was an awareness I hadn't experienced before, and an appreciation for everything small and large. A newfound freedom to live a life of fullness and childlike simplicity.

Now I know more of why Jesus shared with us the importance of becoming childlike, for such is the Kingdom of God. Children don't worry about things like provision and money, because they get lost in creativity and their innocence doesn't even realize they're need for monetary things.

Have you ever had a child turn and say to you, "I need to be diligent in my creativity so that I can produce enough product to pay my bills ASAP!"

No, not with a three-year-old. Why? Because their innocence has shielded their mind from the survival mentality.

When a child is creating something simply for the joy of it, there is nothing to block provision from being manifested. The awesome thing is creativity keeps the mind from being consumed with worry.

◆ ◆ ◆

Worry. The Worn Out Warrior Of Intellect

"Worry is the worn-out warrior who creates a wall
of logic that blocks provision from coming in."

God was reminding me of the power of innocence, and the gift of its royalty in the form of creativity. I now understood a level I hadn't before. He was giving the secret to effortless provision and that was to trust, play and remain like a child. He was showing me that it is completely safe inside his heart to create whatever my own heart desires; for out of it flow the many wonders of life. He was revealing the difference between effort and well-being. He was showing me it's not about what I do to get provision, but more importantly, the DNA of who I am and whose I am. He was showing me the magnetism of an innocent mind engage in its Maker.

I kept thinking about the goodness of who he was as I was being carried through the brilliant colors of the sea. They went on as far as the eye could see. With each passing moment, I could hear the whisper of love saying, "All of the gold and silver are mine and they are yours too." I chuckled with joy every time I saw another sparkling jewel "smile" at me as I passed by many more mountains of jewels and endless treasures floating about in the sea. I was no longer feeling unworthy about money or provision. Or feeling the need to apologize for seeing all of this opulence in front of me and desiring it. I didn't need to because Jesus was playing in it and giving me the approval to do the same.

But as magnificent as all of this extravagance was, my heart just longed to be with his. All of this wondrous beauty and wealth means nothing without playing and laughing with Jesus. Watching him laughing like a child splashing around in the gemstones was all the provision I could ever want. Hmmm, could it be that the provision I had been lacking before was due to my own inability to see the true invitation that Jesus had been offering all along? Could very well be. It's so obvious to me now that he is not the same God who lives in the paradigms of some of the most studied theologians.

Rest is the key to living in union and victory. The current was

now taking me deeper into the sea, and I wondered where I was heading next. Then with one big thrust, it shot me up toward the surface, launching me straight out of the water, and onto the "shore".

"Splat!"

I stuck the landing with both feet into the sand. I looked up and thought, "Whoa! That was a rush! That was better than one of those Flyboard Jet machines you play with in the water! Ha! Ha! Man! This is so much fun!"

◆ ◆ ◆

Right Fish On The Menu

In that moment I thought about all the wonderful things that happened on my journey under the sea. I just stood there for a moment letting my toes sink into the warmth of the sand. It reminded me of when I first stood on the beach in Hawaii with Jesus before we entered the heart. I pondered a little more, and then looked over to my left and noticed Jesus and Swirly sitting in the sand eating something, or at least it looked like they were eating.

Jesus waived me over and asked, "Are you Hungry? It's time to eat" As he winked at Swirly with a smile on his face.

I thought, "Eat? That's odd. Why would we need to eat anything inside the artery? I completely forgot about eating."

"Ok, sure! What are we having?" I said with curiosity, as I walked over to where they were sitting.

"Right Fish! We are enjoying some "Right Fish" together!" Jesus said with joy.

"Right Fish? What's that?" I said with bewilderment.

"Yes! It's Right Fish! You know, fish that were caught on the "Right side" of the boat!" Jesus exclaimed with laughter.

"Ohhh, I see where this is going. I get it! You mean the kind of fish that were caught by the disciples?" I asked.

"You got it! And it's joyfully delish! Want some?" Jesus asked.

"Lol! Sure! I'll give it a try. It smells really good!" I said in mouth watering fashion.

"I cooked it myself on the good ol' Traeger Grill!" Jesus said with confidence.

"Ha! Ha! No way! A Traeger? How is that even possible right now?" I said with a hearty laugh as I took a large bite. "Wow! This is so good!" I said as the "Right fish" melted in my mouth. I could taste the joy and love that went into catching it and cooking it.

"Did I not say that all things are possible to those who believe?" Jesus asked with assurance.

"Why yes, you most certainly did Jesus!" I said with amazement at the site of an actual Traeger Grill.

"I cooked the fish on the Traeger because I know you like them, and they actually do taste better with a little hickory added." Jesus said with a chuckle.

"Why yes, they do!" I said with a smile.

I kept looking over at the grill in awe and wondered how it was being powered. I knew that Traeger Grills need to have electricity in order for the auger to work to pull the wood pellets down into the tray. I looked around the grill for a bit to see where the electrical cord was and where it went. To my surprise it was plugged into a large, crystal-clear diamond that was buried half-way into the sand. I laughed and thought, "Now that is something you don't see every day! I'm gonna leave that one right there!"

Smiling from ear to ear I walked back over to stand next to Jesus. He was staring out towards the sea and looked to be in deep thought. I moved over and stood closer to him to try and see what he was looking at. Just then I felt that familiar tug on my ankle. I looked down and sure enough, it was Swirly trying to get my attention again. He was pointing towards the grill while belly laughing. He just kept laughing and laughing as he pointed. "What are you laughing at Swirly? What is so funny?" I asked as I looked a little closer and noticed some movement over by the electric cord.

"What is happening over there?" I thought.

"Pfft!"

I heard the sand move. "What?" I said out loud. It was a little crab attempting to run off with the diamond that was plugged into the grill! "No way! Ha! Ha!" I shouted as the little crab somehow got the diamond unplugged from the cord and stumbled off into the distance underneath the weight of it. I looked over at Jesus to see if he was going to stop it, but he just kept staring at the sea with a smile on his face. Then he said, "Yeah, he won't get too far. He's gonna realize the magnitude of a fully empowered diamond here shortly."

Shrugging my shoulders, I looked back down at Swirly in wonder of what Jesus was even talking about. But as soon as I thought the thought, I remembered my previous experience on the beach, where the crabs were running away or attempting to run away with the jewels that were laying in the sand. All of the sudden I knew what Jesus meant by what he said. The diamond that was plugged into the grill was different than the others I saw before entering the heart, because this one was sitting in the fullness of its purpose inside the Artery of Creativity. Whereas the others were still diamonds of course, but they were laying there waiting to be empowered with creative purpose.

"You guessed it my friend! It's just like diamonds in the sky! Shine bright like a diamond...do do do do do!" Jesus said while singing the Rihanna diamond song.

"Ha! Ha! Wow! No way! You know that song? Ha! Ha! I just can't! Well? My friends won't believe you even sing that song!" I said with laughter and amazement.

"Yeah well, let's just say I don't sit around singing hymns all day. I love some of them, but I also love other songs as well. I created music, and people have the ability to compose what they want with it. Singing about diamonds in the sky reminds of why I created the stars in the Heavens. Just like diamonds in the sand. They too have purpose. Stars creatively light up the sky to give energy to the dance floor of Heaven, just like the diamond does to the electrical cord on this Traeger Grill to cook a great meal."

Jesus said with one eyebrow raised and a wide smirk on his face to match it.

Have you ever broken your face with a smile? I think mine just did. As I relished this moment, I started to hear dance music playing above me. I looked up and saw lights flashing to the beat of the music. "Ha! Ha! No way!" I started laughing with joy. It was if Heaven was dropping down to join us for a celebration. Swirly was laughing too as he danced around in the sand to the beat of the music. Can it get any better than this? I thought as I looked out towards the middle of the sea once again.

"Look over there. Do you see it?" Jesus said as he pointed out to the ocean.

"I do see something that looks like a boat. Is that right?" I asked.

"Yes, that's right. It's the boat where the "Right Fish" were caught." Jesus said.

"Oh! Ok! Wow! That's amazing! Please tell me more about these "Right fish". I've wanted to know more about the disciples fishing story for years." I inquired with anticipation. (*Jesus was talking about the story in the Bible where the disciples caught a huge haul of fish.*)

"Thank you for asking, because I was going to do just that". Jesus said enthusiasm.

He set his plate of half-eaten fish down by his right foot and began telling me about the fishing story. Swirly jumped up on a nearby rock to listen intently to what Jesus was about to share. I could see he was posturing himself to give Jesus his undivided attention. Even the Prompting of Jesus stands at attention when he speaks. Seeing Swirly become so serious made me quickly realize Jesus was about to say something meaningful that would blow my grid once again.

"Ok, here we go! So, you've heard it said the disciples went fishing all night and caught nothing. That is true. They got into their boat, left shore, and tried to fish like they normally did, but wound up with nothing that night. This is a very typical scenario with people who are skilled in their work but perform it through a left-brain effort. It's kind of like going to school to become educated in a particular area of interest. The more you study and the harder you work to accomplish your goal of getting a degree, the more confident you feel in your intention. After a while, it becomes second nature, and you expect a certain outcome. This is how it was and is with many of my disciples. They become educated in something and then take action with their left hemisphere to develop a methodology that works. But if it doesn't happen to work the same way twice, then disappointment is most likely the outcome.

When the disciples went out to fish that night, they thought they could rely on their tried-and-true method of fishing. They soon found out that formula alone cannot produce what they wanted every time. There is much more to the story. You know me, I am always revealing a higher dimension of a current reality.

Here's what I want you to see...

When frustration and disappointment begin to intertwine with a conditioned, left-brain method, it causes a resistance to fill the atmosphere around that person. It's like pushing against water as you row a boat. The water in front of the boat will be forced out of the way with resistance. But when the boat comes to a rest there is no longer any resistance pushing the water away. So, then what happens? Water now begins to flow back towards the boat that is now at rest.

It's the same way with fishing. When you cast a net into the deep waters of intellect with frustration propelling you forward, then the frequency of that effort begins to work against you. It's called resistance. The disciples were feeling hurt, frustrated, and disappointed at not catching any fish like they normally would do. They actually felt abandoned. Even though hope was present in their right hemisphere, they just couldn't move past what they felt. And what do you do when you feel this way? You default to what you know. Back to what is familiar, and comfortable. They were used to fishing a certain way and they were good at getting results.

Hard work will produce...for a time. But what do you do when that effort no longer gives you the results you're used to?" Jesus said as he dropped his head with compassion remembering their need for change. (*He paused for a moment and then started to weep. He just kept staring at the boat in the water as if he was remembering that precious moment in time with his disciples. I didn't want to interrupt, so I just stood there patiently waiting to hear more. I knew he was in deep thought for a reason. It was like a holy moment. One I'll never forget. To see Jesus standing there with tears running down his cheeks, yet with a smile of hope on that beautiful face was priceless.*)

Brushing the tears from his face he continued, "This is where everything changed for the disciples. Their view of what they thought effortless provision may have looked like, changed forever as they took my word for it. You see, sometimes all of your hard work does not pay off and for good reason. You were never meant to live a life of hardship and formula to begin with. If you were, then I wouldn't have given the example of what ease looked like in the Garden of Eden. I would have simply told Adam to fend for himself by saying, "Keep using that shovel you made Adam! Good luck! Keep applying that formula you developed, you'll eventually shape the Garden into something beautiful with all of that hard work, determination, and sweat-filled labor you've been doing. If you ever do get to the point where you need my help, just let me know when you've had enough, and I'll jump in with the horse and tiller to give you a hand."

Did I ever say that? No, not even when he decided to take another route on his own. I said I would never leave man nor forsake them. It was Adam's decision to take the path of his own logic, which led to his wandering and intellectual ascent. When a person continues to fight for their own way it's like a fisherman trying to catch fish through their own self-effort. There's a hard way to do it and there's an effortless way.

> "Nets thrown into the waters of disappointment,
> intellect, formula, and reasoning, will wind up leaving
> someone exhausted. But effortless pleasure awaits
> all who enter the realm of joyful creativity inside
> the right hemisphere of their playful journey."

The disciples were already feeling loss on several levels when they went out to fish. Whenever you put your hands to something in a state of perceived loss and frustration, then opposition is there to greet you with lots of disappointment. But when you cast your nets into the hemisphere of joy where I reside, magnetism is there to greet you with abundance. Why? Because abundance is the outcome of joy.

Oh yes, there's little doubt that those who engage in hard work

and efforted pursuits will gain wealth and abundance at various levels. But nothing compares to the attraction of Heaven's wealth that is drawn through lighthearted innocence. When you choose to dwell in this truth, innocence is something I smile upon and defend. Remember when I said that if you become like a child, (which is the same as keeping my commands), that your joy would be full? This is that which was spoken. If you align to the playfulness of your authenticity, your joy will be full. And when you live in the fullness of joy, resistance is no longer holding up the bounty.

You see, every living and non-living thing on the planet is made of energy and that energy emits frequency. That frequency is a calling you can consciously tune in to by stilling yourself or having fun playing. Children do this all the time with one another. They do so because they are living out of their right brain functionality having fun creating. Their energy is given to play, because they don't yet know any other way.

Now, think about the time I said, "Let there be light!" Light came into being through my desire. It's the same with everything I've created. You have that same capability. The good thing is fish have already been created, so it's easy to simply receive what is attracted to your desire and feel-good emotion.

When I asked the disciples to cast their nets on the right side of the boat, it was their choice to agree with my words that shifted them out of striving and into receiving mode. Thereby causing a magnetic vibration to flood the waters and call the fish to swim into the nets. In fact, it was that agreement with me that caused a powerful tangibility to occur. It allowed the strength of the "earth" to yield to them in abundance. So much so, they could barely haul in the catch.

How's that for switching channels in your brain from frustration to elation? It's that simple and that powerful. This is why children attract things to themselves all the time. The more they stay in play, the more goodness comes their way." Jesus said with an ear-to-ear grin.

"Ha! Ha! No way!! That is absolutely amazing! Wow! I knew there was way more to that story!" I said jumping up and down with joy.

"Would you like to hear more?' Jesus asked.

"Yes! Of course! So, was it the joy of anticipating there would be fish waiting for the disciples on the right side of the boat that made them power through the hard work of pulling up the nets? What about the strain and stress of pulling in the haul?" I eagerly asked.

"Ok, I get what you're saying, but let me take another bite of fish before I give you an answer. With all this excitement it's made me a little hungry" Jesus said laughingly as he reached for the piece of fish sitting by his right foot.

"Oh! Oops! What's this?" He said as he took a large bite of the fish. He lifted his right hand and pulled a large coin out of his mouth with his fingers.

"Ha! Ha! No way! Is that a coin? Was that inside the fish?" I asked with laughter.

"It sure does look like it eh?" Jesus said with a smirk.

"Ok, now you're messing with me again. Was that really inside the fish?" I asked with a laugh.

"Perhaps, but there's more to that story as well. But first, let me

answer your question about hard work." Jesus said as he wiped his hands off.

"Ok! Awesome! I've been wanting the answer to this question for most of my life. I mean, it's not like I can't work hard when I'm doing something, but the word "hard" makes it sound, well, hard. Isn't there a better way to see work in general?" I asked with somewhat of a hope deferred inflexion in my tone.

"I'm glad you asked me that question my friend. I have been try-ing to answer this question for a long time, but you weren't quite ready to receive the answer until now. Do you know how dizzy I was getting following you around the Tree of Knowledge a hun-dred times?" Jesus said laughingly as he put his arm around my shoulders.

"Ha! Ha! Very funny. Do you know how sick I was getting sitting in that tree eating its rotten fruit?" I said halfway laughing.

"I know my friend, and there is absolutely no condemnation for the experience you've gained through it all. Put it this way, at least you have some distinctive contrast now, right?" Jesus said with a compassionate smile.

◆ ◆ ◆

The Fish That Got Away

Another question for you, "What does a fish and a coin have in common as it relates to fishermen?" Jesus asked.

"Umm, I really don't know," I said.

"When I asked one of the disciples to go fishing to pay taxes, it was symbolic of what he was used to doing as it relates to hard work. Although I made it easy for him to simply walk down and pull the fish out of the water, it was designed to be a moment of contrast for Peter to gauge how far he had come in his understanding of provision with me. He was used to working hard and striving to get the provision he needed before he met me in person. Peter lived with the idea that under Law there was only one way of getting paid and that was through sweat and toil. In his mind, there weren't any other options for provision.

If a person believes hard work is the only way of doing something they don't particularly enjoy, then they'll become frustrated at the level of income it produces. I noticed Peter became a little frustrated when I asked him to go back to fishing to get the money needed to pay the taxes. He couldn't understand why I wouldn't just simply pull a coin out of thin air to pay the bill. It's true, I could have done just that, but if I continued to do it for him, then he wouldn't see the beauty of sonship and effortless provision through his own hands.

Having previously watched me abundantly supply in many creative ways, he could have shifted his mindset to playful creativity while he was fishing and caught the one that was worth not just one, but five coins, which was actually swimming right next to the one that was worth a single coin. If he had caught the "Right fish", a buyer was waiting nearby to offer him five coins. But because Peter was unwilling and unaware of the divine appointment due to his frustration, the magnetism of joy wasn't there to bring them together for the purchase. It was the magnetic frequency of non-resistance surrounding the buyer that hit the wall of resistance residing in Peter's attitude, thereby canceling the abundant transaction.

You see, when you're in a hurry to do the bare minimum because you're frustrated by the request or the bills you're working for, then the joy of creativity is shut off and so is abundant supply. It's not like Peter didn't have my permission to be creative in catching more than one fish. He knew that my nature was easy, and my ways were light. He just chose to catch the first one that took the bait so he could run back with his catch as soon as possible. And that's ok too. Again, there is no condemnation in the process of awakening.

The coin in the fish's mouth parable was an example of showing people the difference between having just enough money to pay the taxes or having more than enough through limitless magnetism.

When you work with a survival mentality inside a system that is built upon the same, then the ceiling of limitation will keep giving you just enough, and sometimes not enough. This is why simply going to work for someone else whose business is built upon a foundation that cannot support limitless creativity, is not the highest way to receive provision. Well-meaning people put in a hard day's work with an attitude of frustration because they know they are being cheated somehow. They know they have untapped potential in their heart that's just waiting to be released, but they don't have the freedom to release it working under a system that does not allow for it.

Peter couldn't feel my Prompting to engage creative flow as he was going to catch the single fish, because he had been conditioned by the Law-fueled Tree of Knowledge mindset for much of his life. And when this kind of conditioning dominates the landscape of your mind, then all you can see are the formulas you've created through it.

The Tree of Knowledge system gives you a fixed income called a paycheck that is built upon a "Caesoric" foundation. It's the rendering to Caesar what is due to Caesar syndrome because the paycheck is gained through left-brained efforting much of the time. It's designed that way to hold people captive to limitation and lack. Which is why the disciples were quick to leave their jobs to follow the voice of creativity empowered by non-resistant love. They couldn't help it. They were compelled to leave because their spirit met its match of creative flow and the full permission to live it.

Abundance comes when there are no limitations. Joy floods creativity to bring up a haul of abundance you could have never imagined when the suffocating ceiling of self-efforted work is removed. Lessons in life can be learned the hard way or they can be caught through joyful receptivity. Either way, contrast will help you to decide how you see provision, and how much frustration you are willing to allow.

Jesus continued...

All of creation speaks of the goodness of love in how it looks, smells, tastes, and sounds. The trees clap their hands, the rocks cry out, and the ocean resounds with the goodness of creative rhythm and flow. They are all alive and flooded with life standing before all of humanity as signposts and reminders of what inspiration looks like. Their only "job" is to remind humanity just how much I love them, and the beauty creativity, when it's fully manifested.

Everyone has been given gifts, and talents to express the au

thenticity of creativeness. In return, that individual, colorful expression reveals who I am in the midst of the "grey". So, when you ask me about "hard" work, I tell you again that nothing is "hard" except that which you put your mind and hands to in misalignment. It only takes a thought to miscalculate and start heading in a direction that makes you feel unhappy, heavy, and frustrated. And it only takes another one to realign to that which is effortless.

When a person puts their hands to something they enjoy they are in-joy, and that playful joy begins to call out to others to come and see what all the excitement is about. Once the crowd gathers, people want whatever you are creating. You cannot help but want to share that creation with the entire world, because of all the fun you are having.

Do you see what happened with the disciples when they received the huge haul of fish? Their joy had such an impact on the atmosphere that the entire cosmos couldn't help but to speak it out to future generations to be transformed by. It's the same with the coin in the fish's mouth and the parable of the talents." Jesus said with a deep contentment in his voice.

I stood there completely dumbfounded at what Jesus was sharing. I fell into the sand on the shore as I felt the love and eternal wisdom pouring out of my best friend. His words made me feel like an innocent child again. I couldn't get enough. I never wanted to leave this place. I wanted more.

◆ ◆ ◆

Buried Treasure

As I mentally descended back to the warmth of the shore from pondering these amazing revelations, I noticed Swirly digging around in the sand next Jesus. It was funny because he looked like a little chihuahua feverishly digging a hole with his "paws" throwing sand everywhere. He was even grunting like a little dog would do as he made his way deeper into the sand. Deeper and deeper he went until he disappeared out of sight.

"Where did he go? What is he trying to find?" I asked.

"Oh, he'll be just fine. He always has a purpose in what he does. He'll be back up shortly." Jesus said as he laughed at the sight.

"Wait for it! Wait for it!" Jesus said teasingly.

Slowly I saw something shiny start to come back up through the opening of the hole Swirly was digging.

"What is that?" I asked.

I waited a little longer to see what this shiny object was. And then I saw it. It was another coin of some kind. I moved over to take a closer look and it was shiny on one side and completely dull and oxidized on the other.

"Ok, this is interesting. I wonder what this is about?" I thought as I watched Swirly pop up behind the coin.

"There you are!" I said laughingly.

"Great job Swirly! I'm glad you found the buried talent. Now let's talk about it." Jesus said with satisfaction.

"Buried talent?" I thought. Ok, I think I know where this may be going. My mind raced to the story of the Parable of the Talents in the Bible. I was excited to hear what Jesus was going to reveal about this.

"This coin was buried a little ways down there, right Swirly?" Jesus asked.

Swirly nodded and even seemed a little winded at having to dig so far down. He was covered in sand and jewel dust from head to toe.

"Ok, let's talk about the talent, shall we?" Jesus quipped as Swirly took a seat next to him.

"You've heard it said that a landowner gave several bags of coins to several employees in whom he trusted and cared for. He had history with those he employed, so it was a natural thing to do. One of them had won the heart of the landowner and was on the verge of being entrusted with much of the estate, due to his camaraderie and wide range of skill. He had grown in his love for his employer but came to know him as more of a friend than a boss. The other employee had the same type of relationship, only he mainly worked outside taking care of the land according to his ability as a groundskeeper. And then there was the one who held this talent in his hand as if it were the last one in the world. He buried right it here in the sand in the Artery of Creativity. The reason the coin was shiny and bright on one side and dull on the other is because it was representative of doublemindedness.

You know the story my friend. Let me ask you, why did the two

employees take delight in doubling the landowner's money and the other did not?" Jesus asked with both eyebrows raised.

"Umm, because they had a better attitude than the other one?" I said with hesitancy knowing Jesus would have more to share about the story.

"That's part of it, but there's more to the story. Two of them came into the fullness of relationship with the employer. Why? Because they understood what it meant to live from the tree of relationship over the tree of knowledge. Therefore, it was their pleasure to help someone they not only worked for but cared for. Because they did, it was their joy that caused creativity to reveal itself in how they invested. But more importantly, they flourished because they knew the heart of the one they served. On the contrary, the one who buried his talent here saw his employer as just that, an employer who had an agenda. He was fearful and skeptical because he grew up eating the fruit of Law and couldn't make the transition to the tree of life paradigm with the owner and the other employees.

In other words, when you live in a mindset of reward versus punishment, then the knowledge you have gained through it, will leave you with a skewed view of others who provide for you. It doesn't matter if an earthly employer has flaws, it's how you view them through the mindset you hold that matters. The two employees saw their employer as more of a relationship than a cruel taskmaster making them work harder for his own gain. This was not the case for the other servant.

You see, when you believe you have to work hard for your own provision, then you'll have a scarcity mentality, and you'll miss the security of creativity that is always standing in front of you. If the two employees saw their employer as a cruel taskmaster, then creative flow would not present itself in such a way that brought increase to their investing. You can't have joy if you feel like punishment is waiting for you if you don't produce. This is what the one servant believed as he buried his talent in fear.

This is why it's so important to be aware of what tree you are actually eating from. The fruit on the Tree of Knowledge will wind up leading you to bury your talent. The Tree of Life mentality on the other hand, causes awareness to ignite the innocence of exploration and possibility in the ability given.

I want to be clear here my friend. I am not the one who was forcing the employees in the story to do anything they did not want to do. I am pleased with my friends whether they create or not. If I wasn't pleased, then it would be about performance and I am not into making people perform, period. The story is about a master and his servants or an employer and his employees, to reveal the difference in how people view their own beliefs about me. One can believe I will punish them for not performing, while the other knows my heart because they spend their time in relationship with me.

I don't send people to hell because they didn't invest their money or their gifting in the earth. In fact, I don't send anyone to hell. People live in their own mental hell bound by a "prison" sentence because of their own beliefs about my nature. This is where many of my beautiful friends shut down, because they believe they don't have any talents to invest or they hold onto them out of fear. (*Jesus took a deep breath as he tried to hold back tears. I could see the compassion in his countenance as he shared about the talents and the lies people believe about his nature.*)

◆ ◆ ◆

Moving Beyond What Others Think

"Fear will keep you digging holes to bury things of value because of skewed beliefs, while joyful creativity gives you limitless returns because love casts out the fear of judgment."

Wow! I can see how fear has held me back in my own life from sharing the fullness of who I know myself to be. How many times have I felt the "Prompting" of the Lord or the familiar tug of "Swirly's" hand nudging me to engage a creative idea, but was too fearful to act because of what others may think about me. What Jesus was showing me was that I not only have the inner courage to live authentically, but that I am one with the very source of all creativity.

This artery has revealed so much. In fact, the entire encounter with the heart of my own humanity has shown me that it's perfectly ok to be the real and genuine me, without fear of judgment.

Effortless provision is a very real reality when we trust the inspiration of the Tree of Life (Christ) within, move beyond the negative memories of the past, and remain teachable inside of our own levels of understanding. Engaging the beautiful flow of our unique creativity is not something we strive to do. It's something we are. It's the child in us that was forced to grow up way too fast.

Heaven's provision is not about engaging in some type of transactionary methodology, so much as it is a relational receiving through the enjoyment of play. Remember, dear reader, when we simply create for the joy of creating, that is when the shield of resistance comes down and the blessings of opportunity begin to overtake us. This is the path of least resistance and the effortless nature of our inner being. It's time to throw away the "Oars of Striving" and allow yourself to be taken downstream through surrender. The kind of surrender that takes you straight into the heart of childlike belief.

I couldn't help but to think about how much this encounter has changed my life, and how much fun this time has been laughing, and listening to the only one who knows me best.

Knowing my thoughts, Jesus said, "Come, my friend, let's go home now. It's time to go back to Eden where life began and where creative flow is always present. For out of your own heart carries the many facets of limitless wonder. I am excited to talk about our next adventure together and the many lives we will touch by you simply being you, and me being me intertwined together in creative authenticity.

Let's go Swirly! We have some prompting to do." Jesus said with joy, as he jumped up from the sandy shore of the artery to head back towards the center of the heart through the Crystal Sea of color.

With tears of love and appreciation flooding my eyes, I watched as he and Swirly walked back out into the color-filled waves ahead of me and disappeared into the deep.

ABOUT THE AUTHOR

John Meyer

John is a husband, father, creator, author and speaker. He and his wife Amy love spending time in nature, creating new things, and having deep conversations about life. They enjoy helping others to awaken to their own authentic creativity through childlike play.

Their mission in life is to take the HARD out work and turn it into effortless creative flow. You can learn more about who they are and what they are currently creating by going to: www.endofeffort.com

**VISIT OUR MEDIA CHANNELS TO
FOLLOW OUR LATEST MESSAGES,
PRODUCTS, AND ADVENTURES**

youtube.com/endofeffort
facebook.com/theendofeffort
instagram.com/endofeffort
web: endofeffort.com

THE SURFING JESUS

My wife Amy painted this picture while I was writing
about Jesus surfing the Maverick Wave.

Made in the USA
Las Vegas, NV
27 September 2021